SAINT MICHAEL
AND THE ANGELS

CREATION

SAINT MICHAEL
AND THE ANGELS

A MONTH WITH
ST. MICHAEL AND THE HOLY ANGELS

Compiled from Approved Sources

"And there was a great battle in heaven, Michael and his angels fought with the dragon, and the dragon fought and his angels: And they prevailed not, neither was their place found any more in heaven. And that great dragon was cast out, that old serpent, who is called the devil and Satan, who seduceth the whole world; and he was cast unto the earth, and his angels were thrown down with him."

—Apocalypse 12:7-9

TAN BOOKS AND PUBLISHERS, INC.
Rockford, Illinois 61105

Formerly titled *The Precious Blood and the Angels.*

Copyright © 1977 by Marian Publications, South Bend, Indiana, under the title *The Precious Blood and the Angels.*

Copyright © 1983 by TAN Books and Publishers, Inc.

Library of Congress Catalog Card No.: 82-62040

ISBN: 0-89555-196-9

Printed and bound in the United States of America.

TAN BOOKS AND PUBLISHERS, INC.
P.O. Box 424
Rockford, Illinois 61105

1983

CONTENTS

TRIUMPH OF THE CROSS

THE PRECIOUS BLOOD AND THE ANGELS

INTRODUCTION

In his book entitled, "The Precious Blood," Father Faber presents the story of the Precious Blood in the picture of a "Procession" which shows us the Blood of Christ going out from the eternal Mind of God, circulating in time and ascending again to Heaven, after having taken on Its way, each one of those creatures of God who owe to It its own beauty and happiness.

"The first visibility of the invisible God," writes Father Faber, "was but an instantaneous flash, and there lay outspread the broad world of angels, throbbing with light, and teeming with innumerous and yet colossal life. The brightness that silvered them was the reflection of Infinite Beauty. From It and because of It they came. Out of It they drew their marvelous diversity of graces. Their sanctities were but mantles made of Its royal texture. They beautified their natures in Its supernatural streams. It seemed as if here the Procession halted for a moment; or perhaps it was only that the sudden flash of light looked like a momentary halt. The new creatures of God, the first created minds, the primal offspring of the Uncreated Mind, were bidden to fall in, and accompany the great Procession. Oh, it was fearful that first sight outside the immense serenity of God! Then, truly, too truly, there was a halt, as if homage and obedience were refused. There is a gleam as if of intorelable battle, and a coruscation of archangelic weapons, and Michael's warcry echoing, the first created cry, among the everlasting mountains. A third of that creation of purest light, has, it is maintained, refused to adore the Incarnate Word, and is flung speedily into the dread abyss, and the ranks close in, and the unfallen light now beams more resplendently with its thinner array than ever it beamed before the fallen fell; and onward the Procession moves."

In this brilliant expose, the eminent writer on the Precious Blood, with a few masterful strokes sums up the history of the angels. "Each angel," he goes on to say, "perhaps had thousands of beautiful graces. To many of them, we on earth could give no name if we beheld them. But they were all wonderful, all instinct with supernatural holiness and spiritual magnificence. Yet there was not a single grace in any angel which was not God's free gift,

7

and which has not also its type and counterpart in the Precious Blood. The Precious Blood would have redeemed them, had they needed to be redeemed or were allowed to be redeemed."

These beautiful lines justify us in seeing an intimate connection between the Precious Blood and the heavenly spirits. As each day of the month of September—which is especially dedicated to the veneration of the angels—we consider their glorious prerogatives, may the knowledge we gather from the meditation unfold before the eyes of our soul, new visions of clearer light, greater love and deeper joy. "The path of the just as a shining light goeth forward and increaseth even to perfect day." (Ps. I, v. 18.)

Queen of Angels

8

DEVOTION TO THE ANGELS IS A MARK OF PREDESTINATION

St. Alphonsus Liguori is often quoted as saying that "devotion to St. Michael and the holy angels is a mark of predestination." This reason alone were certainly sufficient to induce us not to neglect their veneration. On the contrary, we should earnestly strive to cultivate their friendship, in which we shall indeed be blessed, for no earthly friends can compare with them in goodness, in power and in love. St. Denis who wrote most inspiringly of the holy angels, took delight in assuming the title "Philangelus," that is "Friend of the Angels." Let us take to heart the advice of Pope St. Leo the Great, "Make friends with the holy angels" and we shall find in them most loving companions in our earthly exile, our champions against the malice and rage of the devils, our advocates at the judgment seat of God, and our amiable companions in bliss and glory throughout the endless eternity.

But why are the angels so little honored? The answer is that most people, even though aware of their existence, take very little trouble to increase their knowledge, and give the angels no more than a passing thought. To honor and love them, we must first know them. Were we to understand their dignity, their perfections, their close relations with God, their excellence and power, we should be drawn to venerate them and rejoice in the glory which their companionship confers upon us. Were we to remember, furthermore, the affection they bear us and the care with which they guard our souls, we should be inflamed with real love for them.

Moreover, the Church has always practiced and encouraged devotion to the holy angels. All the ancient liturgies make mention of them and of the protection they grant to the faithful who invoke them. The early Fathers express the same doctrine. According to Origen these blessed spirits aid us in all our acts of religion by uniting their supplications to ours. They carry our petitions to God and bring back to us favors and benedictions. 'The angels have care of us poor pilgrims," writes St. Augustine, "they have compassion on us and at God's command they hasten to our aid, so that we, too, may eventually arrive at our common fatherland."

Another reason, not the least important, why we should honor and love the angels, lies in the relationship existing between them and us; an affinity which is based on the same Precious Blood. As Father Faber clearly explains, "the angels needed no ransom; amid their almost countless graces there is no redeeming grace. But, there is not a grace in that sea of graces which could not have been merited for them by the Precious Blood. They, too, sing anthems in Its praise, though not the same anthems as the redeemed. Jesus is Head of the angels as well as men, and it is as Man that He is Head of the angels. Thus the whole of that marvellous world of glorious intelligence, profound gladness, gigantic power and beautiful holiness is a province of the empire of the Divine Redeemer.

Loving worshippers of this Sacred Price of our Redemption, let us be happy to join our voices to the angelic spirits in an everlasting song of praise of the Blood Divine which merited for us and could have merited for them unending joy and bliss in heaven.

Blood of Jesus, Precious Blood,
Praise to Thee for all Thou art;
Fount of grace, the Godhead's shrine,
Source of glory, Blood Divine.
Blood that angel hosts adore,
Would that men would love Thee more,
Blood of Jesus, Sacred Blood,
Praise and thanks for all Thou art,
Home where all find peace and rest,
Be Thou known and loved and blest!

KING OF KINGS

SECOND DAY

NATURE AND FUNCTION OF THE ANGELS

The power and the wisdom of God is not confined to the creation of man and of the material world. Beyond man, millions of creatures exist far more perfect than man, whose perfection varies according to their proximity to the ocean of all perfection. In this superior world, spirits are radiant as the celestial hierarchies of stars; there the angelic choirs shine, the splendor of God blazing in their midst.

"The angelic nature is a whole world of perfection in itself. And this at least we know, that angels are spiritual substances, incorruptible by nature, utterly separate from matter and entirely free from all those infirmities which compass us on every side. They are all brightness and beauty, and their loveliness surpasses all the united charms of earth. Their intelligence is godlike, says St. Thomas, for their knowledge extends to all truths of the natural order, as well as to a great number of the supernatural order. They are acquainted with all the secrets of nature and all that remains most hidden from the greatest minds that ever existed, is intimately known to them. They know without labor countless things at the same time and in an instant of time, unaccompanied with doubt or obscurity. They do not make use of discourse like men, nor comprehend the things they know after our manner—that is by reasoning from one thing to another; they understand everything at a glance, and this is why they are styled emphatically, Intelligences." (Boudon).

They are agile and are often represented with wings to denote their swiftness. They can pass from place to place in the twinkling of an eye, without any intervening lapse of time. Their power and strength also are inconceivable. To sum up all their wonderful qualities, these bright spirits may be called pure and lustrous mirrors reflecting the infinite perfections of God.

The saintly Father Olier says that the angels taken all together represent the Immensity of God by their unlimited number and variety, whilst each choir and each angel in particular mirrors one of the divine attributes, such as God's love, His goodness, His strength, etc. Each angel by the very fact of his creation and existence, must first adore, honor and love a particular divine perfection; at the same time he is predestined to communicate to us something of that special character and grace with which he is endowed. "No two angels are alike; no two are equal. God's perfections are

12

infinite and countless millions of angels reflect these perfections in a divinely marvelous way. No two men, no two women, are identically alike, but the difference between them is relatively slight, whereas the difference between two angels is vast, complete. Every angel is specifically different from the other as one species differs from another . . . The angels are unspeakably lovely, they have no shadow of imperfection, no defects. Nothing on this earth can possibly give us an idea of their resplendent glory. No painter, no poet, no artist ever conceived anything like them. They are living replicas of God's beauty."

Fra Angelico's pictures of the angels excel those of any other artist so that Michael Angelo exclaimed on seeing them: "Angelico must have seen the angels in heaven; otherwise he could never have painted them as he has done." But even Angelico's pictures do not give us the faintest idea of the real angels. St. Bridget, who was favored by God with heavenly visions, tells us that were we to see an angel in all his beauty, we should be so ravished with delight at the sight, that we should die of love. When, therefore, the angels appear to men they take a human form in order not to overawe or confound those who look at them.

But what is of paramount importance to us is that the holy angels seek in every possible way to share with us the immense ocean of love and happiness which they themselves enjoy. Their generosity knows no bounds. We have only to ask for their assistance and favors. Speaking of their ministry towards men, the Catechism declares: "To angels is committed by the Providence of God the office of guarding the human race and of protecting men from any serious harm." And Holy Writ confirms this statment: "He hath given His angels charge over thee, to keep thee in all thy ways. In their hands they shall bear thee up, lest thou dash thy foot against a stone." (Ps. XC, 12).

Unfortunately, far from corresponding with their efforts for our welfare we constantly impede them by our sins and imperfections. Were we to know them better and love them more, and were we more docile to their constant inspirations, our happiness would be unspeakably great. It may be said that the angels are passionate lovers of men. They never cease to do us good, neglecting nothing to secure for us the inheritance of glory which has been purchased for us by the Precious Blood of Jesus. It is indeed an indescrible joy for them when they are certain that the merits of the redemption through the Divine Blood of Christ will not be lost on the souls committed to their care.

THE ARK OF THE COVENANT.

THE EMPIRE OF THE ANGELS

As messengers of God and executors of His orders, the angels exercise a great empire over our souls and bodies and over the material world.

Concerning the power of the angels over the world, the Catechism of Perseverance teaches that "there are angels who impart motion to it. Material creatures inert of their own nature, are set in motion by spiritual creatures, as our bodies are by our souls. Such is the strength of the angels that one of them is sufficient to put the whole planetary system in motion and to carry the most enormous bodies wherever it desires with a rapidity that baffles all calculation." According to St. Augustine, there are angels who preside over every visible thing and over each different species of creatures in the world, whether animate or inanimate. If God were to open our eyes and show us the angels under sensible forms, what wonders we should discover! Let us consider that all the comfort and benefit we derive from earth, air, water and fire, from the heavens from animals—in fact from every creature, comes to us through the agency of the holy angels, who are God's faithful ministers.

St. Thomas incidentally gives us another proof of angelic strength. He teaches that each great star, planet and sun, every heavenly body, even the greatest, has its own Guardian angel to keep it in its course and to prevent any possible aberration. What prodigious energy and power does not such control demand! It is true that the stars and heavenly bodies by the natural direction given them by God pursue their several courses; but these great worlds are material and, therefore, as the Angelic Doctor points out, are liable to decay and deterioration. To prevent disorder and confusion in the thousands of heavenly bodies whirling through space with inexpressible speed, God gives each one, in His all-wise Providence, an angel to keep it in its course and avert the dire calamities that would result were it to stray from its allotted orbit.

Few people think on this when on beautiful, starlit nights they gaze on the heavens and the myriads of stars. "The starry world," writes Father Faber, "is an overwhelming thing to think of . . . Mary's Son is the King of stars." How fitting it would be to salute the countless angels who guard these stars and who look down upon us with love and tenderness.

15

"Whenever we look abroad, we are reminded of those most gracious and holy Beings, the servants of the Holiest, who deign to minister to the heirs of salvation. Every breath of air and ray of light and heat, every beautiful prospect are, as it were the skirts of their garments, the waving of the robes of those whose faces see God in heaven." (Card. Newman).

But the special object of the angels' care is the human race which they are appointed to guard. In the opinion of St. Clement, St. Gregory the Great, Origen and other holy writers, every country, every city, town and village, and even every parish and family has a special Guardian angel. Believing this firmly, St. Francis Xavier invoked the Guardian angel of every country and city in which he preached the Holy Gospel, and when he left one place to preach elsewhere, he never failed to commend to the protection of the holy angels the new congregation he had won to the Faith.

So, too, altars, churches, dioceses and religious institutions have their own Guardian angels. Every church has special angels to guard it from desecration and every altar has thousands of angels to adore the God of heaven and earth concealed in the Most Blessed Sacrament.

According to the testimony of the learned historian, Baronius, angels protected the churches of Constantinople and the palace of the Emperor against the attacks of the Arians. The same historian relates that when the Saxons entered a church dedicated to St. Boniface, they were repelled by two angel-warriors, who appeared in wonderous beauty and strength.

Blessed Peter Faber, a renowned missionary of the Society of Jesus and the companion of St. Ignatius, its founder, brought many souls to God by his work of evangelization in Germany. While traveling through the diocese of his birth, he received innumerable consolations from the Guardian angels of several parishes. On repeated occasions he received most sensible proofs of their protection. Sometimes these holy angels preserved him from the fury of heretics; at other times they rendered souls more mild and tractable to receive from him the doctrine of salvation.

Lastly they guard each one of us. "Every man has a Guardian angel appointed to enlighten, defend and guide him during the whole course of his mortal life. This consoling truth is, next after dogmas expressly defined, one of the best founded in Scripture and Tradition." Even pagans seemed to have retained something of the original Tradition on that subject and one of the earliest Greek poems contains this remarkable passage:

16

Upon the thickly-peopled earth,
In ever ceaseless flow,
Full thrice ten thousand deathless beings
Pass lightly to and fro.

Keepers, unseen, of mortal men,
In airy vesture dight,
Their good and evil deeds they scan,
Stern champions of the right.

To this office of the Guardian angels of men we shall return in subsequent pages. Suffice it to say with Father Faber, that "all these marvels—of the broad world of angels—belong to the empire of the Precious Blood. There is not a corner of God's creation, which is not more or less benefitted by the Precious Blood." Let us then never cease to thank the Divine Blood with our whole hearts for all It means to angels and men.

IN CHARGE OF GOD'S ANGELS

St. Paul expressly states that the specific mission of the angels is to minister to men who have not yet attained the heavenly kingdom: "Are they not all ministering spirits, sent to minister to them who shall receive the inheritance of salvation?" (Heb. I, 14). "Every soul," continues St. Anselm, "is confided to an angel at the same moment that it is united to its body." Tradition cannot, on this matter, be more general, more uninterrupted, or more uniform.

"Although the salvation of our souls is the principal object of solicitude with our tutelar angels, yet they extend their care so far as to procure us the goods of this life also; they preserve us from accidents to which we are all exposed, and deliver us from evils when we have fallen into them. They will carry you in their hands, says the Scripture, lest you should hurt yourselves against a stone; the Lord will send His angels round those who fear Him, and He will deliver them from all their tribulations. The holy angels procure us temporal goods, by preventing the demons from injuring us. 'Our weakness,' says St. Hilary, 'could not resist the malice of the evil spirits without the assistance of our Guardian Angels!' 'God aiding,' adds St. Cyril, 'we have nothing to fear from the powers of darkness, for it is written: The angel of the Lord will encamp round those who fear Him and will deliver them. The Guardian Angels are not content with enabling us to avoid the snares of the devil and turning us away from vice, they also assist us in the practice of all virtues . . . But they have a more special care of the just, in proportion to their fervor in the practice of virtue; so that sin seems to remove them to a distance, inasmuch as it interrupts or diminishes more or less the effects of their vigilance." (Catechism).

"As for the soul, the angels can and readily do act on it, in a manner—now ordinary, now extraordinary—to an extent which is difficult to realize. The understanding owes many precious lights to them . . . Regarding angelic operations on the human will, the universal experience of mankind testifies how many inspirations of good angels are efficacious in leading us to virtue, and on the other hand, how often the suggestions of the wicked spirits are efficacious in leading us to vice. But the good angels disperse the mist of error, lead back the senses to their original purity and produce a kind of internal light in the soul, by means of which it is enabled to see things in their true character. Such are in their nature the admirable creatures whom we call the good angels."

"Wherever we go," writes Cardinal O'Connell in his beautiful pastoral on the holy angels, "this angelic partnership is never interrupted. Heavenly spirits shield us from bodily dangers and minister to us in our temporal needs . . . Intent upon the salvation of our souls, they instruct us, they protect us, they plead for us with God. To every want of the soul through life they minister, that they may assist it to arrive safely at its journey's end. All this they do for us, if we but let them; every help that they can give is ours, if we but welcome them and gratefully co-operate with them.

"Many are the motives which prompt such constant devotion to our interests. These celestial patrons, we know, are close to the merciful Heart of the Redeemer; they understand therefore, His untiring concern for our welfare, and from that inexhaustible Fountain of Love they imbibe the tenderest affection in our regard . . . However, what especially enhances the intensity of their affection is the fact that they have a Divine commission to watch over us, and to be for us here upon earth the instruments of God's mercies. This it is that urges them to sweep down from their golden skies to flash swiftly and joyously through the dim air of this lower world, that they may assure us of their love and be at hand in all fear and trouble.

"And with what admirable solicitude and unceasing watchfulness do these protecting angels fulfil their Divine commission with regard to us! At every moment, though unseen, they are by our side. They never forsake us from the first breath we draw until we have entered into the possession of our eternal destiny. They hover about the babe slumbering in its crib, they guide the timid and untried steps with which childhood and youth enter upon life, at first so strange and at all times so full of perils. They hold out a helping hand to strong and rugged manhood, seasoned by struggles with the forces of evil, and bearing perhaps the scars which the wounds of sin have made. And when the light of life is transformed into the darkness and gloom of age, with its dreams unrealized and its hopes cherished in vain, Guardian angels are near to support the bent form and tottering steps and to banish the shadows of loneliness and sorrow."

"The lives of the saints reveal that many of them had devotion to their Guardian Angels. Some were even privileged with the familiar companionship of their angels and received visible proofs of the services which the holy angels render to those under their charge.

St. Rose of Lima, the first American blossom of sanctity upon whom Holy Church conferred public veneration, lived a life of great purity and innocence. From early childhood she was privileged to hold familiar intercourse with the holy angels. From numerous difficulties and dangers she was delivered by her holy angel and she once declared that her Guardian Angel did whatever she asked him to do.

Pope St. Gregory the Great was tenderly devoted to his Guardian Angel. It was to him that he owed the obtaining of the Papal dignity. During the time the saint was Abbot of a monastery he had built in Rome, his Guardian Angel frequently appeared to him, disguised as a poor merchant, and begged for alms. After he became Pope, St. Gregory adopted the custom of daily feeding twelve poor persons. Among these he beheld one whose virtuous bearing impressed him deeply. Upon inquiring of this person who he was, he received the reply: "I am the poor merchant to whom you gave, besides twelve dollars, the silver dish of your mother. This act of charity which I caused you to perform prepared you for the dignity of high priest. I am your Angel. Fear not, Gregory. God sent me to tell you that you would obtain everything you asked for through my service. As I was the cause of your being raised to the Chair of Peter, I shall also protect and preserve you in this position until death."

MARY RECEIVES HOLY COMMUNION (By Mueller)

"I see the Blessed Mary at Mass, and St. John celebrating. She is waiting for the moment of her Son's presence: now she converses with Him in the sacred rites. She receives Him, to whom once she gave birth."

—*Meditations on Christian Doctrine*

THE NINE CHOIRS OF ANGELS

The angels are divided into nine choirs and form three hierarchies, hence the "angelic world is presented to our view as a magnificent army ranged in the most admirable order."

The first hierarchy is composed of the Seraphim, the Cherubim and the Thrones; the second comprises the Dominations, the Virtues and the Powers; the third is formed of the Principalities, the Archangels and the Angels. Each choir has a different office as will be shown in the following outline, necessarily brief, since the scope of this little work does not permit more. But let us fervently beg each one to share with us the particular grace with which it is endowed.

The Seraphim come first. Their very name means ardor, and they are consumed with the fire of Divine Love of "which they are the created representations." This burning love keeps them ever close to God's Throne and they bear love and light to the lesser choirs of angels. O ardent Seraphim, enkindle in our hearts, by the virtue of the Divine Blood, the sacred flame of the love of God with which you are consumed.

The Cherubim are next. Their name signifies "fullness of knowledge." They are characterized by a deep insight into God's secrets and they truly possess the fullness of the divine science of heaven. They enlighten the lesser choirs of angels and are to them the Voice of Divine Wisdom. O bright Cherubim, instruct us more to appreciate the power of the Precious Blood, in the excellent science of the saints, that we may also praise and glorify God with you.

The Thrones form the last choir of the first hierarchy which is the closest to the Divine Majesty. They are so styled because their main characteristics are submission and peace. God rests upon the Thrones and in a certain manner conveys His Spirit by these angels, who in turn communicate it to the inferior angels and to men. We should pray to the Thrones especially for peace. O Blessed Thrones, obtain for us peace through the Divine Blood, that peace which the world cannot give, which comes from submission to God's will in our regard.

The second hierarchy of angels is more specifically devoted to the management of human affairs. It opens with the Dominations, so called because "they rule over all the angelic orders charged with the execution of the commands of the Great Monarch." Therefore, these bright spirits make known to us the commands of God and their main virtue is zeal for the maintenance of the King's authority. Let us remember them when seeking God's will and invoke them in our perplexities. O holy angels, pray to God for us, that we may ever be faithful to His holy will in all the circumstances of our earthly pilgrimage.

To the choir of Virtues has been confided the duty of carrying out the orders issued by the Dominations. To them is attributed strength and we should seek their assistance in combatting the enemies of our salvation. "It is through them also," says Boudon, "that God governs the seasons, the ·visible heavens and the elements in general, although angels of the lower hierachy have charge of them." Let us therefore have recourse to the Virtues in all extraordinary necessities of mind and body, as well as in times of public afflictions. O mighty Intelligences, help us always, in virtue of the Divine Blood, to accomplish with perseverance whatever duty has been entrusted to us by God's will.

"The Powers," someone has said, "are the favorites among mortals." They are appointed in a special way to fight against the evil spirits and to defeat their wicked plans. "When we see storms gathering either in the Church or in the State, machinations to resist those who are working for the glory of God, extraordinary conspiracies to defeat some great good which is being planned for some diocese, city or country, then it is that we ought to perform frequent devotions in honor of these Powers of heaven, that they may overturn and destroy all the might and miserable plotting of hell." (Boudon). O invincible Powers, in virtue of the Divine Blood, defend us against the attacks of the devil, the world and the flesh and make us victorious against that triple power.

The Principalities preside over the third hierarchy. Their duties are executive in regard to the visible world of men. They also guard the nations of the earth and St. Thomas says of them: "The execution of the angelic ministrations consists in announcing divine things. Now, in the execution of any action there are beginners and leaders; this—the leadership—belongs to the Principalities." We should then invoke them for the protection of our country that it may realize the designs of God upon it. Those who have to exercise any authority should honor these blessed spirits in a special way; they would receive from them graces of light and strength in the discharge of their duties. Sovereign Principalities, in virtue of the Divine Blood, govern also our souls and our bodies, and assist us in the attainment of our eternal destinies.

The Archangels are entrusted with the more important missions to men. They are also given as guardians to great personages, such as the Holy Father, Cardinals, Bishops, Rulers of States, and others who have special work to do for the glory of God upon earth. They protect the Church under the leadership of St. Michael and defend it against its enemies. Let us not forget them when praying for the triumph of the Church, that these celestial spirits may safeguard its interests and watch over our Supreme Pontiff. Noble Archangels, we beg you to aid us always, that profiting by the Divine Blood, we may ever live in faith, hope and charity, and die as true children of our Holy Mother the Church.

The Angels, specially so called, close the last choir of the spirits of light. They are the ordinary messengers sent to men and from their ranks our own guardian angels are usually chosen. They mirror in a very particular way the goodness of God toward us. They are ever ready to go wherever the will of God sends them, and they minister to all, just and sinner alike. They have a true sense of values and they know that to serve God in any capacity is a very great honor. Let us frequently invoke their help as they are most happy to be of service to us. As they are our lifelong companions, we shall speak of them more at length later. Most holy Angels be ever for us the guardians of our safety and salvation, and since we were redeemed by the Divine Blood, obtain for us the grace of final perseverance.

SIXTH DAY

THE COURTIERS OF THE KING OF KINGS

The angels who are not appointed to perform exterior duties are considered God's Courtiers in a more special way, although all the angels without exception, as Our Lord points out "always see the Face of His Father in heaven." Theology assures us that a first glance into the home of the angels will reveal to us countless throngs of bright spirits facing the Throne of their King, the Triune God. They contemplate His divine perfections, basking in the eternal sunshine of heavenly delights. They offer up the praises, the prayers, the good works of mortals. They plead the cause of human beings against the devils, by offering in their behalf the Precious Blood of Jesus. This ministry is exercised above all by the Seraphim, the Cherubim and the Thrones, as being the nearest to God in the celestial realm.

Here on earth we may say that these sublime spirits are represented in these most lofty functions, although in a very imperfect way, by those souls who devote their existence to the praise and glory of God in the contemplative life. To consecrate oneself here below to glorifying God and to cultivating the soul, to meditating on His greatness, His perfections and other attributes, is to reproduce upon earth the life of heaven. It is to lead the life of the angels, who praise their Creator continually and who will praise Him eternally. Souls vowed to the contemplative life, though hidden in the cloister, serve the Church and society effectively. By an austere life of prayer and good works, they make reparation to heaven for the sins of the world. Like the angels, they offer to God the Precious Blood of His Divine Son, to solicit grace and pardon for themselves and their brethren. They pray for the sanctification of nations and plead the cause of all. They call down upon the world the beneficent waves of the Redeeming Blood which bring comfort and forgiveness to suffering hearts and wounded souls. In a word, they imitate the angels who do good to all. Let us often ask the angelic spirits to increase the number of contemplative souls whose hidden mission is so useful to the world and gives such glory to God.

God's Courtiers from the moment of their confirmation in grace found all their joy in the contemplation of the Beatific Vision. This joy must have been immeasurably increased when Christ appeared in His Sacred Humanity and took His place at His Father's Right Hand. Henceforth there would be renewed rejoicing among the angels over every sinner doing penance and whitening his soul in the Blood of the Lamb. And what tongue can tell the glorious scenes that took place in Paradise when, a few years later, Mary the Mother of God was assumed body and soul into heaven and proclaimed Queen of Angels? With what bursts of triumphant song the angelic Courtiers must have welcomed the humble Virgin whom the proud rebel hosts had refused to honor!

A very beautiful story is told about St. Cajetan, who at his birth had been dedicated to the Mother of God by his noble parents. Cajetan led an heroic life of charity and was remarkable for his devotion to our Lady. One Christmas eve, the gracious Mother of God showed her appreciation of his love by placing the Infant Jesus in his arms. "When St. Cajetan was on his death bed, resigned to the will of God, eager for pain to satisfy his love, and for death to attain to life, he beheld the Blessed Virgin radiant with splendor and surrounded by ministering Seraphim. In profound veneration he said, 'Lady, bless me!' Mary replied, 'Cajetan, receive the blessing of my Son and know that I am here as a reward of the sincerity of your love and to lead you to Paradise.' She then exhorted him to patience in fighting an evil spirit who troubled him and gave orders to the choirs of angels to escort his soul in triumph to heaven. Then, turning her countenance full of majesty and sweetness upon him, she said, 'Cajetan, my Son calls thee. Let us go in peace'!" (Butler's lives of the Saints.)

It is the sight of God as He is, the contemplation of the Divine Essence unveiled, the Beatific Vision, as it is called, which has made the angels blessed until now, and will continue to be to them the one source of supreme and perfect bliss for all eternity. They will never weary of it. We weary only of what satisfies our cravings but imperfectly. We can never find true contentment here, because no earthly object and no accumulation of earthly goods fully meets the yearnings of the human heart . . . There is only one object whose possession stills every craving, because it fills to its utmost capacity the whole mind and being of the creature, fulfilling all its desires and setting all its longings at rest. Only the vision of God, the Infinite Good, can bring it peace. No wonder if amid such blissful repose, ages glide by unnoticed and "a thousand years are as a day that has passed."

Whatever else may be the occupation of the angels, they never lose sight of God. They love Him and they sing forever the song of love. Their will is ever one with His and they are at all times full of melody in His praise.

O Angels of Paradise, God's resplendent Courtiers who continually gaze upon the Blood of our Redemption "in Its consummate glory and beautified immortality," we beseech you to intercede for us, that we, too, may attain to that unending bliss and sing with you the eternal song of the Elect, in praise of the Precious Blood which has merited heaven for us.

Father Faber tried to give us a faint glimpse of that beautiful heaven which the angels enjoy with the saints, when he wrote the following verses:

Oh, what is this splendor that beams on me now,
This beautiful sunrise, that dawns on my soul,
While faint and far off, land and sea lie below,
And under my feet the huge golden clouds roll?

See! forth from the gates, like a bridal array,
Come the princes of heaven, how bravely they shine!
'Tis to welcome the stranger, to show me the way,
And to tell me that all I see round me is mine.

There are millions of saints, in their ranks and degrees,
And each with a beauty and crown of his own;
And there, far outnumbering the sands of the seas,
The nine rings of angels encircle the throne.

But words may not tell of the Vision of Peace,
With its worshipful seeming, its marvellous fires;
Where the soul is at large, where its sorrows all cease,
And the gift has outbidden its boldest desires.

I had hardly to give; 'Twas enough to receive,
Only not to impede the sweet grace from above;
And, this first hour in heaven, I can hardly believe
Is so great a reward for so little a love.

THE SEVEN ANGELS BEFORE THE THRONE OF GOD

Let us consecrate this seventh day to the seven angels standing before the throne of God. "They are believed to form a privileged circle most close to Almighty God." Of this favored group the Archangle Raphael expressly stated to Tobias that he himself was one. "I am Raphael, one of the seven who stand before the Lord." (Tob. XII, 15.) Beautifully, Father Faber refers to the same fact when he sings of St. Raphael:

He is glorious midst the angels,
Midst the highest there in heaven,
Standing almost in the furnace,
Of God's selected Seven!

Again in the Apocalypse we find mention of the seven angels in these words: "Grace be unto you and peace from Him that is, and that was and that is to come, and from the Seven Spirits which are before the Throne." (Apoc. I,4.) These seven seem to be the highest Princes of the heavenly court. Although their most important occupation is the contemplation and praise of the Divine Essence, they are also assigned to special duties, for St. Paul expressly states that they are all ministering spirits. The pious Abbe Boudon who has written so well of the angels, would have us invoke these seven Princes of Paradise that they may obtain for us the grace to avoid the seven deadly sins and that they may enrich us with the seven gifts of the Holy Ghost.

In some of his writings, Father Faber quotes the ancient belief that to these seven privileged Princes is confided the guardianship of the seven Sacraments, which he styles the "vases of the Precious Blood." What a consoling picture to behold these seven glorious angels holding aloft these chalices of salvation. "The Sacraments," continues the eminent Oratorian, "while they express a most wonderful part of the Divine Mind, seem also to imply the Precious Blood. According to the economy of redemption, the Sacraments form the system by which the Precious Blood traverses the whole Church, gifts it with unity and informs it with supernatural energy and life . . . They are fountains of happiness to all the earth. Who can tell what songs of human goodness are being sung this hour in the ear of God, because of the joyous inspirations of the Sacraments? Out of Himself there is no beauty like it, unless it be the jubilee of the angels."

Speaking of the happiness which the angels enjoy in heaven and in which the seven holy spirits participate probably in a higher degree, it is said that "everything in the universe is a source of joy to the holy angels. In all they recognize the accomplishment of that which God has fore-ordained; they know, that from all, He derives honor and glory and they rejoice in seeing how He is glorified in all. This is the secret of true contentment; it is because we think of ourselves and not of God, that we are troubled and dissatisfied. If only we could take the angelic view, nothing would disturb us and we, too, should always rejoice."

These seven glorious Princes also exult whenever one of the children of men joins their happy company. They welcome at the threshold of heaven every soul that enters into its eternal reward. The happiness of all derives a fresh accession from each addition to their choirs and their song of triumph rises louder before the Throne of God. Let us imitate their great-hearted charity and draw from the Sacred Heart, the chalice of the Precious Blood, that love which will make us sincerely share the joy and success of our neighbor.

> "Yes, in that Heart divine
> The angels bright
> Find, through eternal years,
> Still new delight."

O bright Spirits, behold my soul, cleanse it in the streams of the Blood that has merited for us every grace, every protection, every help, for time and for eternity. By that same Divine Blood, obtain that I may treasure all Its precious drops offered to me in God's graces and in the Sacraments of Holy Church.

LOVING SUBMISSION OF THE ANGELS

"In their number the Angels are thought by far to exceed in multitude all the men who have ever been or who are yet to be. St. Thomas arrives at the conclusion that they exist in exceeding great number, far beyond all material multitude. Scriptures also frequently refer to vast numbers in speaking of them. Thus in the vision of the Prophet Daniel we are told: 'Thousands of thousands ministered to Him and ten thousand times a hundred thousand stood before Him'." (Spirit World). These expressions merely signify that their number is beyond computation.

Now there might be confusion in heaven, were this limitless multitude without order. But as we have seen the angelic hosts are divided into various hierarchies and choirs, each one having its appointed duties, "not all equal in dignity but all duly subordinated. The Almighty God who maintains so wonderful a harmony between thousands of suns suspended above our heads and rolling in space, maintains also among these celestial spirits, an admirable order and a marvellous subordination."

Their glory is to execute God's orders promptly and joyously and they lose no opportunity of proving their fidelity and devotion to the most gracious and the most perfect of Masters. They are an example to men of loving service and obedience. The Catechism of the Council of Trent commenting on this clause of the Our Father: Thy will be done on earth as it is in heaven, speaks as follows: "We also pray for the form and manner of this obedience, namely that it be directed according to that rule which the blessed angels observe in heaven and the choirs of other celestial spirits follow; that as they spontaneously and with supreme delight obey the divine Majesty, so we may yield a most cheerful obedience to the will of God, in the manner most acceptable to Him."

Would, indeed, there were more resemblance between the inhabitants of heaven and those of earth. This poor world of ours would be much the happier for it. The thought of these bright Intelligences, so far superior to men, becoming our servants, so to speak, in answer to God's will, should stimulate us to a more ready and loving obedience to the designs of Providence in our regard. It should be, as Father Faber writes, "an endless delight to us that they serve God so well while we are serving Him so poorly and that they themselves so abound in love, that they joy in the love of men . . . The dear angels hang and brood and float over this sea of human joys and sorrows, never too high above us to be beyond our reach and more often mingling, like Raphael, their unsullied light with our darkness, as if they were but the best, the kindest and the noblest of ourselves . . ."

Truly wonderful is the goodness of the angels in not refusing to bestow their care even upon those who commit only venial offenses against their Creator, considering the knowledge they possess of the infinite greatness of the Divine Majesty which is insulted thereby. How amazing then to see that they do not abandon even those wretched persons who live in mortal sin, who trample under foot the Precious Blood of the God-Man and are guilty of His death! With incredible kindness they continue to watch over these unfortunate souls and spare no effort in bringing them to penance and reconciliation with God. Let us then return their angelic services by our affectionate gratitude and confidence.

Some one may ask: "Do these great angels really prize our poor love and friendship?" Most certainly. St. Gertrude tells us that one day she was inspired to offer her holy communion in honor of the nine choirs of angels. God permitted her to see how radiantly happy and grateful they were for this act of love. She had never dreamed that she could give them such happiness. This example should encourage us to do the same, especially by offering the Divine Blood in thanksgiving to God for all the beauty and holiness and glory that He has given them. If we do so they will repay us a thousand times over.

The following lines attributed to Thomas A. Kempis speak beautifully of the angels' loving submission and happiness in heaven:

Angel choirs on high are singing,
To the Lord their praises bringing,
Yielding Him in royal beauty
Heart and voice in love and duty;
None that grieveth or complaineth
In that heavenly land remaineth—
Every voice in concord joining
Holy praise to God combining.
Cherubim their reverence showing,
Bowing low, their pinions folding—
God's majestic throne beholding.
Oh, what fair and heavenly region!
Oh, what bright and glorious legion!

NINTH DAY

THE GUARDIAN ANGEL

"Catholic belief," writes Father Husslein, S.J., "does not rest with merely acknowledging the existence of guardian spirits given us by God. It goes further and asserts as of absolute certainty that every human being has its own Guardian Angel . . . In the next place, it is also a universal Catholic belief that not merely every just man, every child of grace, but in fact every single human being here upon earth, whether Christian or non-Christian, whether in grace or in sin, actually remains during its entire life under the care of a Guardian Angel. It suffices to describe this as absolutely certain. Moreover, it is generally held that each human being has its own distinct Guardian Angel not assigned to anyone else." The words of Our Lord also point to this conclusion: "See that you despise not one of these little ones," He solemnly warned His disciples, "for I say to you that their angels in heaven always see the face of My Father who is in heaven."

The ministry of these Guardian Angels consists: 1st, in warding off dangers to body and soul; 2nd, in preventing Satan's suggesting evil thoughts, and in removing occasions of sin and helping us to overcome temptation; 3rd, in enlightening and instructing us and fostering in us holy thoughts and pious desires; 4th, in offering to God our prayers and in praying for us; 5th, in correcting us if we sin; 6th, in helping us in the agony of death, in strengthening and comforting us; 7th, in conducting our souls to heaven, or to purgatory to console us there. It is thus our Guardian Angels watch over us, keep us, lead us. They see in their charges, souls of priceless value since they were redeemed by the Blood of a God.

Although they cannot penetrate the inner sanctuary of human hearts which God has reserved for Himself, they do all they can to help us. However, it is in our power by an act of our free will to expose our intimate thoughts to our angelic companion. And it is to our advantage for such confidence in his enlightened guidance is of great benefit to our soul. After God and our Blessed Mother, he is surely our best friend, and if we really love him, we will have no secrets to hide from him. "We do not sensibly perceive him. We hear no whispered warnings in our ear. Our hands cannot touch him nor our eyes look up to him. Yet invisibly he is with us. From the first moment of life he guards us and he will not have completed his task until as we trust, we shall gaze with him in glory on the Vision of God."

Father Faber also touchingly describes the solicitude of our Angel Guardians: "Ever at our side is being lived a golden life. A princely Spirit is there, who sees God and enjoys the bewildering splendors of His Face even there where He is, nearer than the limits of our outstretched arms. An unseen warfare is waging round our steps, but that beautiful Spirit lets not so much as the sound of it vex our ears. He fights for us and asks no thanks, but hides his silent victories and continues to gaze upon God. His tenderness for us is above all words. His office will last beyond the grave, until at length it merges into a still sweeter tie of something like heavenly equality, when on the morning of the resurrection we pledge each other, in those first moments, to an endless blessed love. Till then we shall never know from how many dangers he has delivered us, nor how much of our salvation is actually due to him. Meanwhile he merits nothing by the solicitudes of his office. He is beyond the power of meriting, for he has attained the sight of God. His work is a work of love, because his sweet presence at our side he knows to be a part of God's eternal creative love toward our particular soul."

"Yes, in him we have an unseen friend and benefactor, an intimate and never failing companion in our journey through life . . . How often perhaps have we almost felt his presence and his power upbearing and rescuing us from danger! How indeed shall we ever repay him for the love that he has shown us!" Let us ask the Precious Blood to be our thank-offering for so great a favor as his companionship, while with boundless faith and tenderest affection we repeat to him those precious words addressed by Cardinal Newman to his own cherished Guardian Spirit:

My oldest friend, mine from the hour
When first I drew my breath;
My faithful friend, that shall be mine,
Unfailing till my death.

Thou hast been ever at my side;
My Maker to thy trust
Consigned my soul, what time he framed
The infant child of dust.

Thou wast my sponsor at the font;
And thou, each budding year,
Didst whisper elements of truth
Into my childish ear.

And thou wilt linger round my bed,
When life is ebbing low;
Of doubt, impatience and of gloom,
The jealous, sleepless foe.

Mine when I stand before the Judge;
And mine, if spared to stay
Within the golden furnace till
My sin is burned away.

And mine, O Brother of my soul,
When my release shall come;
Thy gentle arms shall lift me then,
Thy wings shall waft me home.

OUR DUTIES TOWARDS OUR GUARDIAN ANGELS

In the words of St. Ambrose: "We should pray to the angel who is given us as a Guardian," and St. Bernard justly reminds us of the duties we owe our Guardian Angel: "Reverence for his presence, devotion for his benevolence, confidence in his care. Always remember that you are in the presence of your Guardian Angel," he exhorts his disciples. "In whatever place you may be, in whatever secret recess you may hide, think of your Guardian Angel. Never do in the presence of your angel what you would not do in my presence."

"The great dignity and sanctity of your holy angels makes the duty of reverence an indispensable one for us. Before the great ones of earth, men are very modest and respectful; yet their dignity is incomparably less than that of the lowest of the angels. Therefore we should always conduct ourselves piously and modestly before our holy angel, refraining from every word, gesture or action which could displease or grieve our heavenly friend and guide. This continued remembrance of the presence of our holy angel is also an excellent means of overcoming temptation.

"If we truly love our Guardian Angel, we cannot fail to have boundless confidence in his powerful intercession with God and firm faith in his willingness to help us. This will inspire us frequently to invoke his aid and protection, especially in time of temptation and trial. It will prompt us also to ask his counsel in the many problems which confront us, in matters both great and small. Many of the saints made it a practice never to undertake anything without first seeking advice of their Guardian Angel."

"Beautifully in the poem, 'To My Guardian Angel," the Little Flower illustrates the true spirit of devotion to our heavenly guide and protector. Tenderly she recalls to him how from the high courts of heaven, where he shone as a splendor of pure flame 'before the Lord of endless light,' he had come down to earth to be her brother, friend and helper, ever at her side. Gratefully she recalls how with loving hand he removed the stones before her feet, lest she should stumble in the path, while his face shone ever more brightly, the meeker and kindlier she grew. Then, too, she bethought herself of the needs of others and begged him to visit with her message those most dear to her, to comfort and console them in her stead. She thus sweetly commissions him:

O thou who speedest through all space
More swiftly than the lightnings fly,
Go very often in my place
To those I love most tenderly.

With thy soft touch, Oh, dry their tears,
Tell them the cross is sweet to bear,
Speak my name softly in their ears,
And Jesus' Name supremely fair!

"Above all she desired that he would kindle within her heart his own burning zeal that she might rescue souls from sin, by pouring upon them the dew of Calvary, the Precious Blood of Christ. With his own angelic raptures she would have him unite her poverty and daily crosses, and so present them, fragrant with celestial devotion at the pure Throne of God. Nor did she envy him his glory, for if he looked upon the Face of God, yet she herself might adore Him here below in His Eucharistic Presence and might carry Him within her very breast. Filled with happiest contentment she concludes:

Thine are heaven's glory and delight,
The riches of the King of kings;
The Host in our ciboriums bright
Is mine, and all the wealth pain brings.

So with the cross and with the Host,
And with thine aid, dear Angel Friend,
I wait in peace, on time's dark coast,
Heaven's happiness that knows no end.

"Above all, we owe to our faithful Guardian Angel the most profound gratitude for the numberless benefits he bestows upon us. Always and everywhere he stands at our side, lovingly protecting us, kindly warning us and earnestly exhorting us. In no way can we better prove our gratitude than by obediently following his admonitions and showing a tender, fillial devotion towards him."

When in the state of grace, a soul is a thing of beauty for our dear angel to gaze upon and he rejoices as it becomes ever more and more radiant through the Blood of Jesus. Let us then never sadden our heavenly companion by sin, but should that misfortune happen to us, may we hasten to the fountains of the Precious Blood which will restore to us our former whiteness.

Besides practising a tender devotion to our own Guardian Angel, we ought also to adopt the laudable practice of venerating the Guardian Angels of others. When we meet persons of our acquaintance, we ought at the same time we greet them, also lovingly salute their Guardian Angel. This can be done by an interior act without attracting notice. Or we may make the good intention and renew it from time to time, that as often as we salute anyone, we purpose at the same time to salute his angel. Soon it will become very easy for us to remember these holy angels and we will receive many blessings from them.

May we never forget that an angel of God ever stands by us, whose loyal friendship, Eleanor C. Donnelly recalls in the following inspiring verses:

Thro' world-weary hours and ways, he attends me;
Thro' long murky nights, watches close at my side;
From every evil and error, defends me;
In danger and death, my protector, my guide!

Dear Prince, more than friend, to my interests devoted,
Forgive me my insults, my graceless neglect—
Thy presence oft outraged, thy service unnoted,
Thy pure inspirations resisted or checked!

All else, save my Lord, would thy charge have forsaken,
All else, save my Queen, would have wearied long since;
No love, save thine own, could have suffered unshaken,
Such daring affronts as I've shown thee, my Prince!

After Life's clouded paths, may thine eyes' holy splendor
Enlighten Death's gloom with its comforting ray!
Lead me on to my God, with thy hand firm and tender,
Till, with thee, I may bless Him and praise Him for aye!

THE ANGEL GUARDIAN AT THE HOUR OF DEATH

God having entrusted the care of our souls to our Guardian Angels, these heavenly friends are animated with the sincere desire of procuring us a happy death. There is no means they do not employ to encourage us and to prepare us for it; especially do they urge us to lead good lives. When they see that the moment of death is approaching, they redouble their care and attention. They awaken the vigilance of those who surround us. Our Lord allowed St. Philip Neri several times to see angels suggesting to those who were around the sick the words they should address to them. In fine they spare nothing that we may depart this life only after having "washed our robes and made them white in the Blood of the Lamb."

"We read in the lives of many saints that their holy Guardian Angels were visibly present at their last hour, comforting them in their final struggle, strengthening them against the redoubled attacks of hell, announcing to them the hour of their death and giving them the assurance that they would be heirs of the kingdom of heaven. Not a few of the saints at their death were seen being carried by exultant angels into Paradise. Frequently, too, the holy Guardian Angels have procured for their proteges the grace of a happy death by calling a priest to administer the last Sacraments.

"In the acts of Blessed John Avila of Spain, we find the following incident, the saint himself vouching for the truth of it. In the year 1575, the Rev. Father Cenlenarcs, a member of Blessed John's Community, was awakened one stormy night and requested to take Holy Viaticum to a dying person. At first the priest hesitated and thought to wait until morning, as he did not know the way and the night was very dark. But love of God triumphed over fear and he started out, taking with him two consecrated Hosts. But scarcely had he left the church when two youths of heavenly appearance placed themselves at his right and left side. They held burning candles, which were not extinguished by the falling rain and accompanied the priest to the sick person and back again to the church. When he had placed the sacred Host in the tabernacle they vanished as suddenly as they had appeared. While the good priest was wondering in astonishment at this occurrence, he received a message from Blessed John which contained the words: 'Do not be astonished at what has happened to you this night. It is quite certain that the two youths whom you saw were angels sent by God to reward your zeal . . .'."

They also inspire the sick with good sentiments and their ministrations continue even after death. "One of the most beautiful and consoling features of the Church's teaching concerning the Guardian Angels is the fact that the mission of the holy angels does not terminate with the earthly life of their charges, but only upon the entrance into Paradise of those souls committed to their care." "Assist him, ye saints of God," the Church prays as the soul is separated from the body, "come forth to meet him, ye angels of the Lord, receive his soul and present it in the sight of the Most High." Surely the Guardian Angel must then play an important role. Accompanied therefore, by still other angelic spirits, the Angel Guardian bears up to God the soul of the just at its departure from this life, while he sings:

"My Father gave
   In charge to me
      This child of earth
         E'en from his birth.
            To serve and save,
               Alleluia,
                  And saved is he.

"This child of clay
   To me was given,
      To rear and train
         By sorrow and pain
            In the narrow way,
               Alleluia,
                 From earth to heaven."

—Cardinal Newman.

"Should it happen that at the moment of death a soul in the state of grace is not yet worthy to behold the Face of the Most High, the Angel Guardian conducts it to Purgatory—the place of its purification—and thereafter is most zealous in procuring for it all the assistance and consolation in its power." Most touchingly Cardinal Newman describes the entrance of the soul into its new abode:

"Now let the golden prison ope its gates,
Making sweet music, as each fold revolves
Upon its ready hinge. And ye, great powers,
Angels of Purgatory, receive from me
My charge, a precious soul, until the day,
When, from all bond and forfeiture released,
I shall reclaim it for the courts of light."

And as he takes his leave, the angel sweetly consoles his protege:

"Softly and gently, dearly-ransom'd soul,
In my most loving arms I now enfold thee,
And, o'er the penal waters, as they roll,
I poise thee, and I lower thee, and hold thee.

"Angels, to whom the willing task is given,
Shall tend and nurse, and lull thee, as thou liest;
And Masses on the earth, and prayers in heaven,
Shall aid thee at the Throne of the Most Highest.

"Farewell, but not forever, brother dear,
Be brave and patient on thy bed of sorrow;
Swiftly shall pass thy night of trial here,
And I will come and wake thee on the morrow."

Meanwhile, however, during its shorter or longer sojourn in Purgatory, the Guardian Angel will often visit the soul to bring it relief and comfort. In the writings of the Holy Fathers, it is revealed that the angels descend to the altars of earth, and drawing the Precious Blood of Jesus from the golden chalices during the thousands of holy Masses daily celebrated, they shower it like a beneficent dew upon the flames of Purgatory. "What untold happiness," exclaims Father Walz, "this daily offering of the Precious Blood through the angels is capable of producing in Purgatory. The suffering souls whom we have made blessed spirits in this manner, truly become 'priests' in heaven, and 'reign on earth' according to the words of the Apocalypse, by ministering to our needs through their intercession at the Throne of God."

When at last the soul is freed from every stain and debt of sin, at "Mary's bidding, the Queen of Angels and of Saints, the Guardian Angel will fly with it to the celestial Jerusalem, escorted as the Church so beautifully sings, by the jubilant company of the martyrs and the choirs of angels, all exulting with him, for the crown is won," the Precious Blood has finally triumphed. Happy and blessed shall we be, if by our devotion to and love of our heavenly companion, we deserve to be particularly assisted by him at our last hour. May he offer for us then to the God of mercy, the Divine Blood, our ransom and our passport to heaven's eternal joys.

TWELFTH DAY

THE SPIRITS OF DARKNESS

Until now we have studied "the presence in our midst of spirits of light, innumerable and invisible, doing the commands of God and protecting us from ill. But other spirits, too, there are inhabiting the air about us and their purpose is to compass our eternal undoing."

"All the angels," teaches the Catechism of Perseverance, "were created in the state of innocence and justice, but they were no more impeccable than man. Being free, they had, like men, to undergo a trial. The Beatific Vision and immutability in good, were the recompense which they should gain by the proper use, with the assistance of grace, of their free will. God, therefore, subjected them to a trial. Every trial to be meritorious, must be essentially costly or painful." What was the trial of the angels? It is generally held that the mystery of the Incarnation of the Word—of God made Man—was proposed to them for their adoration.

"At this revelation," continues the Catechism, "the pride of Lucifer, one of the highest angels, rebelled. He cried out: 'I protest. Is my throne to be lowered? I will raise it above the stars . . . It is I and no other that shall be like the Most High!' One third of the angels of the various hierarchies answered: 'We also protest'.

"At these words an archangel, no less brilliant than Lucifer, cried out: 'Who is like unto God? Who can refuse to believe and to adore that which He proposes for the faith and adoration of His creatures. I believe and I adore.' The majority of the celestial hierarchies answered: We also believe and we also adore.' Such was the great battle that took place in heaven and of which St. John speaks in these terms: 'There was a great battle in heaven; Michael and his angels battled with the dragon, and the dragon fought and his angels.'

"These few words contain treasures of light. In them, and in them alone, is found the real origin of evil. Punished as soon as guilty, Lucifer and his adherents, changed into horrible devils, were precipitated into the depths of hell, which their pride had dug for them.

"Here let us, with humble gratitude, admire the wide difference which Divine Mercy placed between them and us. The door of penance, through the merits of the Precious Blood, is open to men during the whole time of their life, while the bad angels found themselves immediately after their fall in the state in which sinful men will find themselves immediately after their death. The eternal damnation of the reprobate angels, like that of men, consists in the loss of the beatific intuitive vision and in the pain of fire. They have suffered this punishment since the moment of their fall, as sinners suffer it from the moment of their death."

At first glance it appears that God was more severe with the angels than with men. But it is obviously not so, when we consider that their nature is so much superior to ours. Their sin was committed with clear knowledge and with a determination of will unknown to us and was not followed by repentance. This thought should increase our appreciation of the Divine Blood which is ever ready to cleanse us from our sins, especially in the Sacrament of Penance, and restore to us the friendship of God, denied to the fallen angels.

THIRTEENTH DAY

THE ABODE OF THE SPIRITS OF EVIL

"It is a divine truth that these spirits of evil are invisibly present on earth. They inhabit the atmosphere about us and frequent the haunts of men: their homes and shops and marts and places of pleasure. They are busy not merely in person, but also through their agents, whom they are able to control with but little effort. Thus St. John in setting down the message God had given him for the Bishop of the Church of Smyrna, mentions the devil, when he describes the persecution that he predicts will be carried on there against the Christians by their fellow men. 'Fear none of those things,' he says, 'which thou shalt suffer. Behold the devil will cast some of you into prison that you may be tried: and you shall have tribulation ten days (an expression indicating indefinitely a short but bitter period of persecution). Be thus faithful until death and I will give thee the crown of life.' (Apoc. 11, 10)." (The Spirit World About Us.)

We see therefore that "the habitation of the fallen angels is hell and the air that surrounds us; but let them be in hell or in the air, their pain is always the same, for they everywhere carry hell about with them. Such is the teaching of all the Fathers and all the Doctors of the Church . . . With his usual penetration, St. Thomas discovers the reason for the double abode of the fallen angels. 'Providence,' says the Angelic Doctor, 'conducts man to his end in two ways: **directly** by leading him to good—this is the ministry of the good angels, and **indirectly,** by exercising him in the conflict against evil—it is becoming that this second mode of procuring the good of man should be entrusted to the bad angels, that they may not be altogether useless in the general order. Hence for the latter, two places of torment: one, by reason of their fault, is hell; the other by reason of the exercise which they must give men, is the cloudy atmosphere that surrounds us. Now the business of the salvation of man will continue till the Day of Judgment; till then, therefore, will continue the ministry of the good, and the temptation of the bad angels. Hence, until the last day of the world, the good angels will continue to be sent to us and the bad to inhabit the lower strata of the air. But after the Day of Judgment, all wicked men and angels will be in hell and all the good in heaven'." (Catechism of Perseverance.)

With good reason therefore does St. Peter warn us: "Be sober, be watchful, for your adversary the devil, as a roaring lion, goes about seeking someone to devour." (Peter I, V, 8). Lucifer is the name under which the leader of the rebel angels is frequently referred to. **"Helel,** is the Hebrew word, derived from **Halal,** 'to shine'. It applied to him before his fall, since by many he is believed to have been the very highest and so most splendorous of all the angels." (Spirit World). It further appears from the Sacred Scriptures that not merely then, but even now, Lucifer may claim a certain superiority over the fallen angels as actually possessed by him. In their combined hatred of God the evil spirits still acknowledge Lucifer as their chief. They have not lost their natural powers, however fallen and depraved, and they recognize the need of leadership among the forces of evil in their efforts to work harm to souls.

We must remember that they are essentially spirits, as swift as thought, penetrating everywhere and pursuing us everywhere; nothing remains closed to them. They are ever in contact with us. We must resist them strong in the faith and in the power of the Precious Blood, shed to obtain victory over this deadly foe. May we purify our souls more and more in this Divine Blood which will drive away the angel of darkness and preserve us from spiritual death.

TEMPTERS OF MEN

As we have seen the devils hate men and continually plot their ruin. They are envious of the creatures redeemed by the Precious Blood of the God-Man whom they refused to adore, and destined to fill the places left vacant in heaven by their fall. Therefore they cease not to molest us in every way in their power. Unfortunately, "the empire of Satan is extended over all who are in the state of sin and so deprived of the sanctifying grace of God."

"These wretched spirits,' says Boudon, "do their utmost to discover God's designs in a soul, with the view of misleading it and drawing it aside from its appointed vocation or duties. Their temptations are as varied as the individuals whom they tempt. They often throw a veil over the evil which resides in unlawful pleasures; and on the other hand, they conceal from men the good which sufferings contain. They allow men to perceive only what is painful in them, for the purpose of tempting them to impatience, weariness, despair and murmuring against the dealings of God's Providence . . . Whenever they approach they cause trouble, despondency, sadness and confusion, and if they cannot make men the companions of their misery hereafter, they endeavor at least to make them share their wretchedness in the present life.

"It does not follow that the men whom Satan rules may not enjoy the utmost worldly distinction and respect. The prince of darkness, even Shakespeare remarked, is a gentleman. More than that, such men may often profess the noblest motives, or assume an air of sanctity that might deceive the elect. 'For Satan himself transformeth himself into an angel of light,' St. Paul warned the Corinthians (II Cor. XI, 14). St. Ignatius was not an idle dreamer, but a shrewd and divinely aided student of the spiritual life. He well understood the nature of that invisible spirit world about us. In his meditation of the 'Two Standards,' he pictures Lucifer, the mortal enemy of our human nature, summoning together upon this earth, innumerable devils, and dispersing them, some to one city, some to another, and so on throughout the world, not omitting any province, place or state of life, or any person in particular."

"Thus the constant occupation of the bad angels is to tempt man, in order to frustrate the ends of the Incarnation. Not content with destroying our soul by sin, Satan brings upon us all the temporal evils in his power. The devils not only hate man in his person, but they also detest him and attack him in his goods and in the elements necessary for his existence and security. A great portion of the evils that afflict us come from these malevolent spirits. In union with other groups of men, even pagans, the Church has always believed in the dreadful power which God has left to the devils over creatures, and in the use which they make of this power to injure mankind. Hence in the Church we find prayers, exorcisms, blessings on creatures, particularly on those which are to serve for the administration of the Sacraments and the general requirements of Religion." The Sign of the Cross and the devout use of holy water are in particular two very effective means of driving away the evil spirits.

Here again we come under the benignant influence of the Precious Blood of Jesus which through the Church furnishes us with the weapons to combat the avowed enemy of our salvation. Let us make use of them in temptations, but above all let us invoke that Divine Blood directly, and also the Queen of Angels, who will not fail to assist us in our hour of need.

THE ACTIVITY AND STRENGTH OF THE WICKED SPIRITS

St. Theresa was wont to say that "great courage is required in spiritual warfare," and this is very true since our enemies are not only terrible in strength and numerous beyond conception, but also ever active, day and night, ever alert to work our ruin. "The devil," says St. Thomas, "has a certain power over man from the very fact that the latter is subject to original, or even to actual sin. Consequently, it is fitting that before Baptism, the demons should be cast out by exorcisms lest they impede man's salvation." That expulsion, he further explains, is significant by the breathing of the priest on the one to be baptized. The blessing and imposition of hands is to bar his return, and the anointing with oil signifies the ability to fight against the demon. "The Church," he concludes, "uses words of command to cast out the devil's power, for instance, when she says: 'Therefore, accursed devil, go out of him'." (Summa, St. Thomas.)

"What we have said of the agility and strength of the good angels applies also to the demons. Let us add only that the power of the devil is limited by the Divine Wisdom, so that they cannot do to us, nor to creatures in general, all the evil that they would. Accordingly, God never permits them to tempt us beyond our strength. With the assistance of grace we can always resist them, and by the victories that we gain over them, advance the work of our sanctification and increase our merits." (Catechism.)

"Their rage against us," writes Boudon, "is accompanied with such strength that as we read in Job (XLI., 24) there is no power on earth which can be compared to it, and that the devil fears no one. All mankind united could not resist him without the special assistance of heaven, and millions of soldiers in battle array would be to this spirit like a little chaff which is scattered before the wind. Therefore it is that these angels of darkness are called in Scripture (Eph. vi, 12; ii.2) 'powers,' and that they are styled princes and rulers of this corrupt world, the greater part of men being brought by sin into subjection to their detestable tyranny.

"Add to their fury and strength a countless number of malicious artifices which they employ to seduce us, accompanied by such subtle and wicked inventions, that the wisest have been deceived by them, and the most enlightened struck with blindness. The lapse of ages serve only to render them more expert in deceit; hence it is that the later heresies are generally the most subtle. The temptations they employ become every day more dangerous . . . Christ styled satan "a murderer from the beginning." This then is an enemy whom men have had from the beginning of the world, and for six or seven thousand years he has never ceased to busy himself day and night in laying ambushes for them everywhere. St. Anthony one day saw the world full of snares—the air, the earth, the sea and all the other waters . . . This enemy has darts and arrows prepared to let fly in all sorts of places and against all sorts of persons.

"Now if this be so, let us consider with a little attention the dangers to which we are exposed, having such enemies to contend with, and let us at the same time reflect what we ourselves are who have to fight against such forces . . . If we would but let ourselves be guided by the light and movement of grace, we could do all things in Him Who is our strength. 'Resist the devil,' teaches the Divine Word, and he will fly from you'." Let us place all our confidence then in Christ and in His Blood which has merited for us graces of courage and strength to fight our enemy. "It is true our crown is not yet won. The spirits of evil are busy about us. The world and our own concupiscence, no less than the devil are here to tempt us. The combat at times is fierce, but if our souls are humble, heaven fights on our side—and think of the reward!"

Having washed our robes in the Blood of the Lamb, we shall deserve to hear those words of the Apocalypse: "He that shall overcome, shall be clothed in white garments, and I will not blot his name out of the book of life, and I will confess his name before my Father and before His angels."

PROTECTION OF THE GOOD ANGELS AGAINST THE DEVILS

"While the activity of the devil is not to be minimized," writes Father Husslein, S.J., "neither are we to fall into the mistake of ascribing all temptations to him. And on the other hand, we must not exaggerate his power . . . With the advent and death of the Savior the power of Satan was greatly limited. To this period the commentators generally ascribe those words of the Apocalypse: 'And I saw an angel coming down from heaven, having the key of the bottomless pit, and a great chain in his hand. And he laid hold on the dragon, the old serpent, which is the devil and Satan, and bound him for a thousand years (XX.I,2). The text quoted does not mean that the temptations of the evil spirits were to cease during that time, but that Satan's power at all event was to be greatly limited. The thousand years, of course, are not to be taken literally, but as indicating a great period of time . . . When that long period should have passed, Satan was for a brief time to be allowed to exercise his activity again in an extraordinary manner here upon earth: 'And after that he must be loosed a little time' (XX.3). And then shall come the end.

"But in the meantime, until that moment comes, our struggle here below continues. Good angels as well as bad take part in it. We are not left to fight our battles alone." Once more quoting Boudon: "The God of heaven is more desirous of our salvation than hell is furiously bent on our destruction. As He thoroughly knows our powerlessness, in the excess of His divine mercy, He gives succor proportionate to our weakness. His eyes are lovingly intent upon defending us. He sends us the blessed angels of His heavenly court, by an order of Providence which the Church styles 'wonderful,' to uphold us in the battle which we must fight against these powers, whose strength would infallibly overwhelm us without so special a protection . . ."

To enjoy this protection, however, we must never wilfully expose ourselves to temptation. The devil who shows himself so formidable to our human nature is really a coward when we face him bravely, by the example of a good Christian life. Cardinal Newman thus explains this thought in the following verse of his famous "Dream of Gerontius":

"And therefore, is it in respect of man,
Those fallen ones show so majestical.
But, when some child of grace, angel or saint,
Pure and upright in his integrity
Of nature, meets the demons on their raid,
They scud away as cowards from the fight."

With all the good angels on our side, we have more with us than against us. "This truth is very sweet and well fitted to console us in all our troubles. Know also that one single angel of heaven is stronger, in the power he receives from God, than all the devils united. Remember moreover, that all these blessed spirits keep watch in our defense with a goodness beyond all imagination, and that the devils have the greatest fear of them, even more than they have of the saints, excepting the Mother of God. The reason is, that the good angels having fought generously for the cause of God against these apostates at the time of their rebellion, they merited a strong empire over them." (Devotion to the Angels.)

Let us take courage, therefore, and while confiding in the protection of our heavenly companions, let us also thank God whose loving kindness thus provides for our eternal welfare. Let us daily purify our souls in His Precious Blood for

"The ministers of wrath divine
Hurt not the happy hearts that shine
With those red drops of His!"

And often invoke the heavenly companion at our side:

"Bright Spirit, whom the Lord of Love
Didst send me from the realms above,
To guard and cherish, love and guide,
Thy presence let me not forget;
Thy promptings heed, lest I regret
False joys that led my steps astray
From thy benign and guarded way.
Dear Angel, keep me ever true
To God, your Master, and to you."

SEVENTEENTH DAY

GUARDIANS OF CHILDHOOD

"Referring now to the time when first its Angel Guardian is appointed for a human being, we often hear it said that his ministry begins with the birth of the child. But this need not be taken too literally. We may say with the very best of authority and for excellent reasons, that it really begins with the very first moment of human life itself. In the words of St. Ambrose: 'Every soul at the moment it is infused into the body, is entrusted into the keeping of an angel'." (Spirit world.)

The angels are indeed ours "from conception to glory," and it has been truly said that maternal love is the nearest approach to angel love. As these blessed spirits are so closely united to us, devotion to them ought to be part of every Christian household. Parents should cultivate it in themselves and in their children. Family joys would be sweeter if shared with these gracious angels, and in their turn they would repay the affection shown them with untold spiritual and even temporal benefits. What mother has not noticed the narrow escape of one or the other of her children from an imminent danger, probably without thinking that it may have been through the intervention of its faithful Guardian. And when trials and crosses come, as they do in everyone's life; when God sees fit to take to Himself one of the little ones, the angels will be there to pour the balm of consolation upon all, and to comfort the sorrowing mother.

"In a poem entitled "Comforted," Emma A. Lente describes in her exquisite way the experience of a child-soul as it is taken up by its Angel Guardian and led, amazed through the streets of the Heavenly Jerusalem, until it sweetly rests in Mary's arms. Imaginative as the verses are, they describe the mother-love of Mary for a pure child soul:

"The angel took the little child,
And bore him past the shining ranks
Of singers and of harpers, past
The golden streets and lilied banks,
Unto a quiet restful place,
Where Mary sat, with wistful eyes
And tender smile and outstretched hands,
To welcome him to Paradise!

"He was so small and mother-lost.
So dazzled, and so half-afraid,
He could not bear the bliss of heaven,
Or view the hosts in white arrayed,
Until the clasping, loving arms,
And gentle voice dispelled his fears,
And dimmed the memory of pain,
And dried the last faint trace of tears.

"He nestled close against the heart,
The mother-heart where Christ once lay,
And felt the blessedness of peace
Balm all his hurts and griefs away;
And Mary sang until he smiled,
And rocked him till, with life elare,
He faced the wonders and the joys
And splendors of his high estate!

"What joy for the Christian mother who has given up her child to God, to know that at Mary's heart it is only waiting to be restored to her, in a happiness a millionfold more keen than all the sorrows of the parting here! That, also, is one of the comforting thoughts which the Angel Guardian speaks to the bereaved mother, till in the light of faith, the rainbow of new hope plays, glorious through her tears." (The Spirit World.)

Children bear a close resemblance to angels on account of their innocence. But we need not envy them too much, since the Precious Blood is ever at our disposal to restore to us our original purity, should it be tarnished by failings or even by sin. "In the holy Sacrament of Penance, Jesus Christ has prepared for us a laver of His own Blood, to which we have free access to cleanse our soul from every defilement . . ." and to which the Church invites us in these words taken from her divine Office:

> Henceforth, whoso in that dear Blood
> Washeth, shall lose his every stain,
> And in immortal roseate beauty robed,
> An angel's likeness gain.

"How comes it," writes a pious author, "that the angels are so little known and loved? Simply because many whose duty it is to teach this most important doctrine are gravely negligent in fulfilling their obligation.

"First of all Christian mothers should instil deeply into the minds of their children a clear, vivid and abiding sense of the presence of their dear angels. It is not sufficient to give them vague, hazy, insufficient notions of these Blessed Spirits, nor is it enough to teach them to say a short prayer at morning and at night to their Angel Guardians. They should devote much time and much attention to this all important subject. Children must be taught constantly from their tenderest years to have a real love and friendship for their angels, to have boundless confidence in them. They must be accustomed to feel and realize the personal presence of their angels, to call on them in all their fears and troubles. How much better this would be than that the children should have their heads filled with foolish fears of ghosts and goblins as so frequently happens.

"Mothers who impress on their children this great lesson confer on them inestimable blessings during all the long years of their lives. On the other hand, if they neglect this duty or make light of it, they do a great wrong to their dear ones for they deprive them of the best and most powerful friends." (All About the Angels.)

Finally, the office of angel-guardian has in some way also been conferred upon Christian parents, and the heavenly Guardians ought to find in them their most powerful and faithful allies. May they imitate the fidelity of the angels in fulfilling the holy task of rearing their children for whose immortal souls they will one day have to render an account. Untold graces will be their reward, as the remembrance of their heavenly companion will also incite the children to greater love and respect for their parents. "Never let us imagine," says Father Husslein, S.J., "we can outgrow in stature or in years, our need for the daily and more frequent recital of that perfect little prayer to the Guardian Angel which we learned at our mother's knee:

> "Angel of God, my Guardian dear,
> To whom His love commits me here,
> Ever this day be at my side,
> To light and guard, to rule and guide'."

And this other sweet supplication at the close of day:

> "Good-night, my Guardian Angel
> The day has sped away;
> Well spent or ill, its story
> Is written down for aye.
> And now, of God's kind Providence
> Thou image pure and bright,
> Watch o'er me while I'm sleeping,
> My Angel dear, good night!"

ST. RAPHAEL, GOD'S PHYSICIAN

Holy Scripture introduces us to only three of the glorious Princes of heaven by name. They are: St. Michael, St. Gabriel and St. Raphael. We shall speak of each separately, beginning with the last mentioned.

St. Raphael whose name signifies "Medicine of God," seems to be at the head of the angelic medical staff. His reputation as physician and as guide of travelers is due to the story in Holy Writ which relates how he brought healing to the elder Tobias, released Sara from being molested by the devil and gave to the youthful pilgrim in his charge, safety, guidance and most noble companionship. We have only to read of the services he rendered Tobias to love this bright spirit of heaven fervently. Let us briefly go over some of these events.

"At the time of our story the Jews were held in captivity by their enemies. Among the captives was a holy and just man called Tobias who lived with his wife and only son, also called Tobias. His daily prayers and acts of charity towards his neighbor made him very pleasing to God, who as we shall see, gave him in return an exceeding great reward.

"Tobias the elder, wishing to secure the future of his wife and son, and being now blind, was forced to send his son on a long and perilous journey to recover a sum of money which he had lent to a friend. It was most important that the youthful traveler should have a trusty companion. Quite unexpectedly a most eligible companion appeared and declared himself ready to start at once. He gave his name as Azarias. This God-sent friend proved to be a wise and sagacious counsellor. Conferring favor upon favor on the young Tobias, he filled his heart with admiration and gratitude.

"Once when Tobias was attacked by a great fish, his guide came to his aid, and at his bidding, Tobias extracted its gall, heart and liver which later proved to be of great medicinal value. Next, this admirable guide and companion negotiated a most happy marriage for his young protege, securing for him a beautiful and holy wife. This was a marriage made indeed, in heaven. Leaving Tobias with his bride, he went himself to Rages, the city of the Medes, and recovered the money they had come to seek.

"In a word, thanks to the wisdom of Azarias, Tobias returned home rejoicing, full of the good things which his guide had obtained for him and inexpressibly grateful for the services he had rendered him. Boundless, too, was the joy of his dear father and mother, who had been anxiously awaiting his arrival. Their happiness increased when they learned of the inestimable favors done by his guide.

"Yet another unexpected consolation awaited them when young Tobias anointed his father's eyes with the gall which he had extracted from the fish, and the old man recovered his sight.

"And now Tobias took his son aside and asked him, 'What payment shall we make to this heaven-sent companion of thine?' 'Payment?' answered he, 'why what reward can ever suffice for all the services he did me? He it was that escorted me safely, going and coming, recovered the debt from Gabelus, won me my bride, engaged the gratitude of her parents, rescued me from the fish's onslaught and to thee restored the light of day. Through him, we have been loaded with benefits, is it possible to make any return for all these? Do this, father, at least, ask him to accept half of all the wealth that has come to us.'

"So both of them, father and son, beckoned him aside and would have prevailed on him to accept half of their new-found wealth. But he bade them give their thanks to the God of heaven. "To him," he said, "offer your praises for all men to hear. He it is that has shewn mercy to you. When thou, Tobias, wert praying with tears, when thou wert burying the dead, leaving thy dinner untasted, I, all the while, was offering that prayer of thine to the Lord. Then because thou hadst won His favor, needs must that trials should come and test thy worth . . . I am the angel Raphael and my place is among those seven who stand in the presence of the Lord."

"Upon hearing this, they were both mazed with terror and fell down trembling, face to earth. Peace be with you, the angel said; do not be afraid. It was God's will, not mine, brought me to your side; to Him pay the thanks and praise you owe . . . And now the time has come when I must go back to Him who sent me; give thanks to God and tell the story of His great deeds. With that he was caught away from their eyes and no more might they see of him."

Father Faber had a very special and tender devotion to this glorious Archangel as evidenced by the following illuminating and inspiring dedication of his book, "Growth in Holiness":

St. Raphael is the angel of peace, of health and of joy. "Joy be to thee, always," was his salutation to Tobias. He is the angel sent in God's Providence to guide and guard, to heal and save. So it is that he forever typifies the watchfulness, tenderness and helpful affection of our own Guardian angels. For that reason we look on him with a particular affection.

"He is special in his beauty;
Like unto him there is none;
Tender, patient and pathetic,
Dear St. Raphael stands alone.

"O thou human-hearted Seraph!
How I long to see thy face,
Where in silver showers of beauty
God bedews thee with His grace!

"But I see thee now in spirit
Mid the Godhead's silent springs,
With a soft eternal sunset
Sleeping ever on thy wings."

(FATHER FABER.)

Oh, St. Raphael, Medicine of God, Angel of happy meetings, of peace and of joy, we beseech thee, cure our infirmities of soul and body in virtue of the Divine Blood, source of all healing graces.

THE VIRGIN MARY AND ST. GABRIEL, THE ARCHANGEL

"Strength of God"

Be still, ye clouds of Heaven!
    Be silent, Earth!
And hear an Angel tell
    Of Jesus' birth.

While she, whom Gabriel hails
    As full of grace,
Listens with humble faith
    In her sweet face.

Hail Mary! lo, it rings
    Through ages on;
Hail Mary! it shall sound,
    Till time is done.

(A. A. PROCTER)

ST. GABRIEL, GOD'S AMBASSADOR

The name "Gabriel" has been interpreted "Strength of God." Of the three archangels mentioned in Holy Scripture, St. Gabriel appears to be the King of heaven's chief Ambassador, fittingly endowed with dignity, graciousness, knowledge and discretion. And of all the embassies on which he was sent, the greatest was to announce the wonderful mystery of the Incarnation and the mighty work of the Redemption through the shedding of the Blood of the Incarnate Word. "He it was, who at the Annunciation first spoke those words to Mary which ceaselessly reecho round the earth: 'Hail, full of grace, the Lord is with thee, blessed are thou among women' (Luke I, 28). And he it was who there adored with her the Word made flesh to dwell among us." (Spirit World.) He was, we may say, the first Adorer of the Precious Blood on earth, and the first to pronounce the sweet name of Jesus, Savior. He is also considered our Blessed Mother's Guardian in a very special way. We cannot honor Mary by devoutly reciting the prayer that is most pleasing to her, without at the same time honoring the glorious Archangel who was God's instrument in her exaltation. Their names are linked in heaven and on earth.

> "O blessed Gabriel! Tongue of God!
> Sweet-spoken Spirit! Thou hast showed
> To us the Word made man;
>
> "He bade thee break His silence here;
> The tale thou told'st in Mary's ear,
> His coming scarce foreran.
>
> "O Voice! dear Voice! the ages hear
> That Hail of thine still lingering near,
> An unexhaustable song . . ."
>
> (FATHER FABER)

Though his name is not expressly mentioned, we may well believe what tradition tells us that it was St. Gabriel who announced to the Shepherds on the hills of Bethlehem the birth of our sweet Lord, and that it was he who led the multitude of blessed spirits who sang around the crib the heavenly song: "Glory to God in the highest and peace on earth among men of good will." It was he also who consoled dear St. Joseph in his sorrows, and accompanied the Holy Family in their flight into Egypt. And now, in addition to these ancient celestial assignments, St. Gabriel has recently been proclaimed Patron of radio and television by Pope Pius XII.

Lastly, St. Gabriel is looked upon as the angel who comforted Our Lord when He suffered His Bloody Agony in the Garden of Olives. Father Walter Elliott has written inspiring pages on this consoling angel. He says in part: "In that hour the highest angel could not vie with the meanest child of Adam as a comforter of Jesus. Never did He feel so much a man as when He began to sink deeper into man's wickedness and woes. Here then was a new sorrow disguised even in His comfort. For not only did He crave comfort direct from His Father and yet must be content with an angel's instead, but next to His Father's, He craved sympathy from His own kind, His own flesh and blood, His chosen men, and an utterly different comforter was given Him—the while that the Apostles slept and waited . . . Yet, notwithstanding all this, the angel's coming was a gracious boon from His Father.

"For now there suddenly burst upon Jesus a vision of blessed peace. The devils are gone . . . who have been tormenting Him. Oh, what a difference—this gentle being, and just as strong as gentle, full of brightness and affection, all beaming with hope, and peace, reverence and sympathy. How sweet a visit, how welcome a comfort. Hope rose in His Heart, though we hardly dare say joy . . . If we would speak of perfect kindness, we call it angelic; or perfect peace, we call it heavenly. Thus heaven vouchsafed to Jesus an interval, however brief, of its own gentle kindness, deep peace and rest. The angel strengthened Him and Our Redeemer rceived at least a passing comfort from this most affectionate and reverent herald of celestial peace. He merited our eternal thanks for comforting our champion in the direst moment of His awful conflict.

"Christ knew that the only comfort possible for Him was within the gift of men alone, that is to say, their willingness to suffer with Him. But when the angel was come, and before he vanished away, our saddened Redeemer thanked Him lovingly, very grateful for His affectionate ministry.

"Meanwhile, how deep the awe of the angel. How profound from that hour his reverence for our human nature, which in his Divine Master, he saw forming one person with the deity itself, and which he knew, even in the lowest grade of humanity, was being ransomed at such a price. There is much joy in an angel's office of helping sinners to repentance. What joy then, is this angel's, since the foremost penitent of the whole race is here, the one whose contrition is the foundation source of every penitent's saving grief, and it is his unique privilege to attend Him and console Him."

"These are the proofs," concludes Dom Gueranger, "which St. Gabriel gives of his deserving his beautiful name, "Strength of God." God has employed him in each stage of the great work in which He has chiefly manifested His power; for Jesus, even on the Cross, is the Power of God, as the Apostle tells us. The whole human race is indebted to thee, O Gabriel! Blessed messenger of our Redemption whom God selects as His minister when He would show His power, we beseech thee, offer the homage of our gratitude to Him that thus sent thee."

"Angel of strength, 'twas thine to see
The pang of love's Gethsemane,
Thy pinions hovered o'er the form
Of prostrate woe, though in the storm
    That shook the sea
    On Galilee
He stood a Master to defy
The fiercest rage of earth and sky.

"Must I, too, fall beside the press
That yields the cup of bitterness;
Must I within the garden prone
Taste life and living death alone—
    O Angel mine,
    Give strength divine,
That I, love's agony may know,
Because my God hath willed it so."

(RANDOM VERSE)

GOD'S MARSHAL

TWENTIETH DAY

ST. MICHAEL, GOD'S MARSHAL

"Hail, bright Archangel, Prince of heaven!
Spirit divinely strong!
To whose rare merit hath been given
To head the angelic throng."

We begin today the novena preparatory to the Feast of St. Michael, the most brilliant of the angels mentioned in Holy Writ, and "one of the foremost jewels in the crown of God's glorious creation." For nine consecutive days, then, we shall meditate on this most beautiful Prince of heaven, consider his special duties towards men, and the assistance he gives us at all times.

Holy Church gives to St. Michael the highest place among the angels, for she refers to him as "Prince of the heavenly hosts." She tells of the glories of this great Archangel in several portions of her Liturgy and keeps two feasts in his honor. One of the inspiring antiphons for his festival points out: "The Archangel Michael is set over Paradise, and is honored by the citizens of heaven. He repays with blessings the honor shown him by the faithful and his prayer leads us to the kingdom of heaven." St. Michael appears chiefly as the Head of God's armies, champion of the people of God in the Old Testament, and mightly guardian of God's chosen flock under the New. "Fittingly he is represented in art as the angel warrior, the conqueror of Lucifer, setting his heel upon the head of the infernal foe, threatening him with his sword, transpiercing him with his lance, or prepared to chain him down in the nethermost abyss whence he shall nevermore issue after the last day

"The war carried on against the Woman and her Child by the Dragon and his angels is described in the twelfth chapter of the Apocalypse. By that Woman is meant in the first place the Church of God, but in a symbolic sense Mary, too, is signified who bore Christ, and whose children are all the faithful begotten by her and Christ in them. All these the Dragon would wish to destroy. In his persecution of the Church, Satan can know of neither rest nor surcease. It is carried on by him and his followers, now in one part of the world and now in another. It is constantly active round about us. It is waged with diabolic cunning and fury. Science, literature, art, and every human achievement are impressed into its service.

All this would be inexplicable, did we not know its history and its instigator, the devil, who was a liar and a murderer from the first, Satan, the old serpent.

"In the midst of that chapter of the Apocalypse, to which I have referred above, Michael and his angels are suddenly intro- duced in a great battle fought by them against the Dragon and his angels. 'And there was a great battle in heaven' (XII, 7). This event with all its mysterious significance, will most probably take place toward the end of the world. 'And that great dragon,' says St. John, 'was cast out, that old serpent who is called the devil and Satan'." (The Spirit World.)

St. Michael never ceases to wage war against his enemy and ours. Lucifer, whom he once vanquished in the dim and distant ages, and the verdict of that battle will never be reversed. No harm can come to the children of God, who place their trust in the Precious Blood, and in St. Michael, the "standard-bearer of salvation," who ever stands as a firm and impregnable wall against the fiercest at- tacks of the evil one. There is happiness also for us in the thought that the most exalted among the bright spirits of heaven owes all his gifts and glorious prerogatives to the same Divine Mercy to which we are indebted for our salvation. Let us praise the Sacred Price of our Redemption for all Its magnificent graces, and con- gratulate St. Michael on the glory that is his. "How beautiful are thou, O Michael, in thy heavenly armour, giving glory to the God whose enemy thou overcamest!"

ST. MICHAEL'S LOYALTY TO GOD

"The very name of Michael urges us to honor this glorious spirit; it is a cry of enthusiasm and fidelity, for it signifies: 'Who is like unto God?' Satan trembles at hearing this name, for it reminds him of the noble protest wherewith the bright Archangel answered the call of the rebel angels. Michael proved his strength and prowess when he fought the great battle in heaven." From that hour he has been known as "Michael, the captain of the armies of God, first Prince of the holy city, to whom the other angels yield ready obedience. They most willingly and gratefully recognize his supremacy, for after God, they owe to him their perseverance in grace and their eternal happiness. With loving submission they receive from him their various offices. They are attentive to his slightest wish, because they recognize in his commands and regulations the will of God, their sovereign Lord and King.

Thus does God honor and reward in heaven him whose zeal saved the greater portion of the heavenly court from destruction. Next, we hear his praise from no less an authority than his brother Angel, St. Gabriel, who speaking to the Prophet Daniel says: "Michael, who is your Prince," and "Michael, who is one of the first among Princes." Let us look upon this blessed Prince of heaven with holy joy, for he deserves our highest veneration. As St. Gabriel, God's Ambassador, was the first to adore the Precious Blood in the Incarnate Word, upon earth, so was St. Michael Its first adorer in heaven. St. Michael humbly submitted to the trial given the angels and manifested his allegiance to his Divine Master, by an act of profound adoration and fidelity. His fearlessness and fortitude aroused the courage of the faithful angels who rallied to his standard, repeating with one accord his noble cry: "Who is like unto God?" St. Michael and his faithful followers won a glorious victory.

A like triumph will St. Michael win in behalf of all those who place their confidence in him. More than ever in this present age do we need his assistance. "Open and secret revolt against God and His Church, the spirit of criticism, unbelief and immorality are rampant. The haughty and insolent boast of Lucifer, 'I will be like the Most High!' is re-echoed today throughout the world. Puffed up with their discoveries and their progress in material science, men are loudly proclaiming their self-sufficiency and denying the existence of a Supreme Being. Governments and secret societies plotting against God and striving to blot out from homes and schools, from offices and factories, all traces of Christianity, show plainly under whose standard they are assembled. Never before in the history of the world were the rights of God so blasphemously mocked and denied, or the rights of men so arrogantly asserted, as they are today.

"As a remedy against these frightful evils, we are urged to invoke the aid of that glorious Prince of heaven who rendered all glory to God by conquering Lucifer and casting him into the abyss. 'In our times,' writes Cardinal Mermillod, 'when the very foundation of society is shaken in consequence of having denied the rights of God, we must revive the veneration of St. Michael and with him raise the victorious cry: 'Who is like unto God'?"

Three centuries ago St. Francis de Sales wrote: "Veneration of St. Michael is the greatest remedy against despising the rights of God, against insubordination, skepticism and infidelity," vices which are perhaps more prevalent now than in any previous period of history. Let us then with confident trust, invoke the aid and the protection of this mighty Archangel whose shield bears the inscription: "Who is like unto God."

O holy Archangel, may we be ever faithful to God as thou wast. Pray to Him that we, too, may love Him, our common Lord and Master; then shall we be invincible. Be our shield and armour that at all times and in all places we may always defend the honor of the Most High.

ADORATION OF THE INFANT SAVIOUR

TWENTY-SECOND DAY

VENERATION OF ST. MICHAEL

Holy Church recognizes the exalted dignity and power of St. Michael by the veneration she pays to him. He has moreover, been honored from the earliest times and in many countries, as is evidenced from the writings of the Fathers. Under the Old Law, the Archangel was the Guardian of the Hebrew Nation, as the following words found in the Book of Daniel indicate: "Michael, the great Prince who standeth for the children of **thy people,**" now, the Prophet's people, were, of course, the Jews. And again, "It is accepted as without doubt, that the angel of the Lord who was assigned the Israelites in the days of Moses, to guide them through the desert and bring them in to the idolatrous nations whom it was God's will to destroy through them, was the same great Michael. 'Behold I will send My angel, who shall go before thee,' the Lord said to Israel." (Ex. xxiii, 20.)

After the death of Moses, according to an ancient Jewish tradition, referred to in the Epistle of St. Jude (1,9), St. Michael contended with Satan over the body of the Prophet. In obedience to the command of God, St. Michael concealed the tomb of Moses from the people and also from Satan who wished to disclose it to the Israelites in order to seduce them to the sin of idolatry.

St. Michael was God's confidant in His designs of mercy and justice towards His chosen Nation. "Finally, it was this great Prince who came to the aid of the Israelites and rendered the army of Judas Macchabeus victorious over his enemies. Even to this day, the Jews invoke the holy Archangel Michael as the principal defender of the Synagogue and their protector against their enemies. On the Feast of the Atonement they conclude their prayers with this beautiful invocation: 'Michael, Prince of mercy, pray for Israel, that it may reign in heaven, in that light which streams forth from the Face of the King who sits upon the throne of mercy'."

Under the New Dispensation, the position of St. Michael, "was to be enlarged and glorified. He is today Champion of the entire Catholic people." From the earliest Christian ages, the practical devotion of the people has attributed to him numberless spiritual and temporal blessings. The Emperor Constantine, grateful for the victories gained over his enemies which he attributed to the protection of St. Michael, built a magnificent church near Constantinople in honor of the Archangel, which he called Michaelion. It became a place of pilgrimage and many sick and infirm were cured in it by the intercession of St. Michael.

It is related that in Rome also, churches were built dedicated to St. Michael as far back as 494. During the pontificate of St. Gregory the Great, a terrible pestilence depopulated the city of Rome. The Sovereign Pontiff ordered a penitential procession during which he himself carried a statute of the Blessed Virgin. Eighty persons died in the ranks of the procession itself. Still the Pontiff continued the prayers. When they arrived at the bridge crossing the Tiber, they heard the songs of angels in the skies. Suddenly above the castle of San Angelo, St. Michael appeared in gigantic size. In his right hand, he held a sword which he thrust into the scabbard. At the same moment the pestilence ceased.

"In other parts of Christendom, this devotion took root only by degrees, and it was by the holy Archangel's appearing to men that the Faithful were prompted to have recourse to him. These apparitions were local and for reasons which to us may seem of secondary importance, but God who from little causes produces great effects, made use of them whereby to excite Christians to have confidence in their heavenly Protector."

O holy Archangel, protect us and obtain for us in virtue of the Divine Blood, that we may be victorious over the enemies of our souls and enjoy with you the happiness of heaven.

ST. MICHAEL, DEFENDER OF CHRISTIANS

St. Michael has appeared at different times to those who needed help and invoked his aid. A well authenticated example is his assisting St. Joan of Arc in the extraordinary Divine mission, given her to aid the French king restore peace and prosperity to his kingdom and expel his enemies from its shores. Again, in France, he appeared on Mont Michel, where there still exists a famous Sanctuary consecrated to the Archangel.

In Italy it is related that the holy Archangel showed himself to the Bishop of Siponto, on Monte Gargano in the kingdom of Naples where a beautiful church was dedicated to him. In this apparition, "St. Michael intimated to the Bishop that the place was under his protection and that it was his will that God should be worshipped there, in honor of himself and the angels." This became a place of great devotion and attracted many pilgrims.

But apart from the extraordinary cases in which the great Archangel deemed it necessary to appear visibly to the eyes of men, he is ever invisibly active in helping every individual Christian and all Christian nations. We are indeed fortunate in having so powerful an advocate! God gave him a compassionate love for men, and there is not a single soul that escapes his notice. More than ever in our present age, do Catholics need the aid of St. Michael in order to remain steadfast in the Faith. Unbelief has carried its insolence to the very limit and boldly proclaims that there is no God. It is our duty to be faithful Catholics, to confess our Faith openly and energetically and to preserve a glowing, invincible love for Jesus Christ.

Let us never forget that Satan does his utmost to destroy mankind. In a thousand ways he plots and wars against God and tries to usurp His throne. On this subject, the following instruction given by Our Blessed Mother to Venerable Mary d'Agreda, is worth quoting: "My daughter," she says, "by no power of human words wilt thou in this mortal life ever succeed in describing the evil of Lucifer and his demons against men, or the malice, astuteness, deceits and ruses, with which, in his wrath, he seeks to bring them into sin and later on to eternal torments. He tries to hinder all good works . . . All the malice of which his own mind is capable, he attempts to inject into souls. Against these attacks, God provides admirable protection if men will only co-operate and correspond on their part."

Among the means provided by God for our protection, is the ready recourse we may have at all times to the strengthening Blood of Christ. "This Blood," declares St. John Chrysostom, "has the power to drive away the evil spirits and to draw to our side the good angels, aye, the King of Angels, and to blazen the way to heaven." Fortified by the Precious Blood, let us place ourselves under the leadership of St. Michael and unfurl everywhere the banner of our Faith, without fear of godlessness. If Satan tries to induce us to sin, and promises honors, riches, happiness on conditions that we omit a good work, or commit an evil deed, let us ever oppose the tempter with the energetic words: Who is like unto God? God is my only treasure, my highest Good, His Blood is upon me, and "though I walk through the valley of the shadow of death, I shall fear no evil . . ." If in time of temptation, we have the courage to rebuke the evil one and call upon the assistance of our leader, St. Michael, the enemy will surely be put to flight. But if we wish to enjoy the great Archangel's protection, we must also imitate his virtues, particularly his humility and his zeal for God's glory.

"O great St. Michael, take us 'neath thy shield,

Thy mighty power in our favor wield!"

ST. MICHAEL AND THE ANGELS AT MASS

It is said that St. Michael presides over the worship of adoration rendered to the Most High and offers to God the prayers of the faithful symbolized by incense whose smoke rises towards heaven. In fact, the liturgy presents St. Michael to us as the incense-bearer, standing beside the altar as our intercessor and the bearer of the Church's prayers before the throne of God. "An angel of the Lord stood near the altar of the temple, having a golden censer in his hand, and there was given to him much incense, and the smoke of the perfumes ascended before God." (Offertory, Mass of St. Michael.)

At the beginning of Holy Mass, his name is mentioned in the confession of faults made by the priest at the foot of the altar, and by the faithful in turn. At the offertory, in Solemn High Mass, the priest implores the blessing of the Almighty upon the oblation through the intercession of St. Michael. And during the Canon of the Mass, after the Consecration, the priest prays God to command that the oblation be borne by the hands of His holy angel to His altar on high. The angel here referred to is doubtless the Archangel Michael. With loving solicitude he watches over the Precious Blood, that no accident may occur, and also over all the tiny particles which may fall from the consecrated Hosts at the time of Holy Communion, that they may not be lost or desecrated.

But St. Michael is not alone present at the Holy Sacrifice of the Altar. Christian tradition assures us that innumerable angels also assist at Mass. St. John Chrysostom, among others, states that "When Mass is being celebrated, the Sanctuary is filled with countless angels who adore the Divine Victim immolated on the altar." Besides the guardian angels of the faithful who are present, thousands of heavenly spirits assist at Mass, reverently worshipping their Lord and God. With what sentiments of profound veneration do they not adore the Precious Blood being shed anew upon the altar! It is the self-same Blood that was shed on Calvary, but with this difference, that then It fell upon the ground and stones, whereas in Holy Mass, It is applied to the souls of those present. The efficacy of the Mass is so wonderful, God's mercy and generosity are then so unlimited that there is no moment so propitious to ask for favors as when Jesus is born on the altar. The angels know this full well and come in throngs to adore their Divine Master and make their petitions at this hour of mercy. What an example for us! Whenever we attend Holy Mass, therefore, let us unite with St. Michael and the holy angels, "and place our offerings and petitions in their pure hands, to be presented to the Most High, that He may receive them graciously and pardon our indevotion for the sake of the devotion of the celestial spirits with whom we associate ourselves. It was revealed to St. Mechtilde that three thousand angels from the choir of Thrones are ever in devout attendance around every Tabernacle where the Blessed Sacrament is reserved. Doubtless a much greater number are present at Holy Mass, which is not merely a Sacrament but also a sacrifice." And we read in the revelations of St. Bridget: "One day when I was assisting at the Holy Sacrifice, I saw an immense number of Holy Angels descend and gather around the altar, contemplating the priest. They sang heavenly canticles that ravished my heart, Heaven itself seemed to be contemplating the great Sacrifice. And yet we poor mortals, blind and miserable creatures, assist at Mass with so little love, relish and respect!" Do Catholics ever think of this amazing truth, namely: that at Mass they are praying in the midst of thousands of God's angels?

Let us beg St. Michael and his angels to impart to us a greater realization of the infinite value of the Mass, "where Christ spiritually sprinkles the souls of the faithful with His Blood. St. Mary Magdalen de Pazzi says of this spiritual sprinkling: 'This Blood when applied to the soul, imparts to it as much dignity as if it were decked in a costly robe. It imparts such brilliance and splendor that couldst thou behold the effulgence of thy soul when sprinkled with that Blood, thou wouldst fall down to adore it.' Happy the soul adorned with such beauty! Let us go to Holy Mass often, that we may be sprinkled with this adorable Blood and our soul arrayed in rich apparel which will render us glorious forever in the sight of the angels and the saints. The Catholic Church owns no greater, no more costly treasure than the Precious Blood of Jesus Christ; for a single drop of this Blood, which is united to the Second Person of the Blessed Trinity, outweighs in value all the riches of heaven and earth."

Let us remember also that one Mass heard during life is of more benefit to the soul than many heard for it after death, and that every Mass will go with you to Judgment and plead for pardon. They will, moreover, shorten your Purgatory and win for yourself a higher degree of glory in heaven. How pleasing to God is the frequent attendance at Mass, is well illustrated in the following gracious little story:

A poor farmer was wont to attend daily Mass for many years

of his life. He was crossing the snow-covered fields one cold morning on his way to church, when he thought he heard foot-steps behind him, and turning, he saw his Angel Guardian bearing a basket full of beautiful roses which exhaled a delightful perfume. "See," said the angel, "these roses represent each step you have taken on the way to Mass and each rose represents also a glorious reward which awaits you in heaven. But far, far greater are the merits you have acquired from the Mass itself."

The thought of the priceless advantages that are to be derived from devout assistance at Mass, ought to be a stimulant for us to hear it not only on Sundays, but also on week days, whenever possible. Should illness or some other serious reason prevent us from doing so, let us send our Guardian Angel in our stead with the following prayer:

"O holy Angel at my side,
Go to the church for me,
Kneel in my place, at Holy Mass,
Where I desire to be.

"At Offertory, in my stead,
Take all I am and own,
And place it as a sacrifice
Upon the Altar Throne.

'At holy Consecration's bell,
Adore with Seraph's love,
My Jesus hidden in the Host,
Come down from heaven above.

"Then pray for those I dearly love,
And those who cause me grief,
That Jesus' Blood may cleanse all hearts,
And suff'ring souls relieve.

"And when the priest Communion takes,
Oh, bring my Lord to me,
That His sweet Heart may rest on mine,
And I His temple be.

"Pray that this Sacrifice Divine,
May mankind's sins efface;
Then bring me Jesus' blessing home,
The pledge of every grace."

ST. MICHAEL, HELPER OF THE SICK AND THE DYING

From what has already been said it is evident that the function of military guardian is not the only one assigned to St. Michael in the mind of the faithful at various periods of history. In the early Eastern Church the function of healer was in a special manner attributed to him. It is quite naturally associated with his general solicitude for the welfare of the charge committed to his protection." Tradition relates that in the earliest age, St. Michael caused a medicinal spring to spout at Chairotopa near Colossae, and all the sick who bathe there, invoking the Blessed Trinity and St. Michael, were cured. Still more famous are the springs which St. Michael is said to have drawn from the rock at Colossae. The pagans directed a stream against the sanctuary of St. Michael to destroy it, but the Archangel split the rock by lightning to give a new bed to the stream and sanctified forever the waters which came from the gorge.

At Constantinople, likewise, St. Michael was the great heavenly physician. The Christians of Egypt placed their life-giving river, the Nile, under the protection of St. Michael. In Rome, as we have seen, his reputation for healing became known when he caused the cessation of a mighty pestilence in the days of St. Gregory the Great. Many other instances of a miraculous nature also illustrate his power of curing ills which he shares with St. Raphael, "The Medicine of God." Though military captain of the Church of God, St. Michael, nevertheless, interests himself profoundly in all the great public happenings of his people, and particularly in the calamities befalling them, while he does not overlook their private petitions for aid under any circumstances. Let us therefore have recourse to him in times of sickness and if it is God's will that we should experience his help, he will most certainly come to our assistance bearing to us the healing graces of the Redeeming Blood.

But if in His merciful designs, our heavenly Father has decided to call us home, St. Michael continues his angelic ministration till he sees us safely through the eternal portals. For not only during life does the glorious Archangel defend and protect souls, he is especially their advocate at the hour of death. "He assists at every deathbed," writes Dom Gueranger, "for his special office is to receive the souls of the elect, on their quitting the flesh. He, with loving solicitude and princely bearing, presents them to the

Light Eternal and introduces them into the House of God's glory. It is holy Church herself that tells us, in the words of her Liturgy, of these prerogatives of the great Archangel. She teaches us that he has been set over Paradise and that God has given him the charge of leading to heaven the souls of them that are to be received there." When the last hour of our earthly career draws near and we are confronted by that awful moment when our soul must leave the body which it has loved so much, to pass through the narrow portal of death, satanic hosts like raving lions will make a last attack upon our souls. But we need not fear, if during life we have had devotion to the Precious Blood and have been faithful in venerating St. Michael and in imploring his aid for the hour of death. "Devotion to the Blood of Jesus," says Father Walz, "would seem to have this wonderful distinction, that it dispels the fear of death and fills us with hope and confidence to meet our Judge. 'Having therefore, brethren, a confidence in the entering into the holies by the Blood of Christ' " (Heb. X, 19.) "The Blood of Jesus Christ," adds St. Bernard, "speaks with trumpet tones, not of the judgments of God, but of His mercies." And the great St. Thomas Aquinas calls the Precious Blood the key to the heavenly Paradise.

In that hour of supreme need, the invincible Archangel, ever-ready to assist the faithful soul, will come to our aid with his glorious hosts and battle for us. He will cover us with his strong shield and lead us safely through the midst of our enemies. It is therefore a very commendable practice daily to invoke St. Michael to lend his assistance at the hour of death. Many are the faithful clients of St. Michael who have experienced his help in that hour.

Among the writings of St. Alphonsus Liguori, we find the following account of St. Michael's assistance at the hour of death: A certain Polish nobleman had for many years led a wicked life. When the hour of his death approached, he was filled with terror and tortured by remorse of conscience over his former recklessness, so that he was reduced to utter despair. No amount of exhortation or encouragement had any effect upon him; he refused absolutely every spiritual consolation.

This unhappy man, however, still had some veneration for St. Michael and God in His mercy permitted the holy Archangel to appear to him in his last struggle. St. Michael encouraged him to repentance and said that he had prayed and obtained for him sufficient time to regulate the affairs of his soul. Shortly afterwards, two Dominican priests came to the house, saying that a stranger had sent them. The sick man recognized this as the work of St. Michael. He confessed his sins amid tears of repentance, received

Holy Communion with touching devotion and breathed forth his soul with every indication of being truly reconciled with God.

"Thou, O Michael," we read in the Liturgical Year, "art the Protector of our souls in their passage from time to eternity. During this present life, thine eye is upon our wants and thine ear open to our prayers. Though awed by the brightness of thy glory, we love thee, dear Prince of heaven and we live happy and contented beneath the shadow of thy wings. In a few years perhaps, our holy Mother the Church will be performing her last rites over our lifeless remains; she will pray for us, to our Heavenly Father, that we may be **delivered from the lion's mouth and that the standard-bearer, St. Michael, may bring us into the holy light.** (Mass for the Dead. Offertory.) Watch over us now, O holy Archangel, lest we should then not deserve thy protection." See to it, dear St. Michael, that having been sprinkled with the Precious Blood of our Redeemer received in Holy Viaticum, we appear clothed with the royal robe before our Judge.

> "Thee, Michael, thee,
> When sight and breathing fail,
> The disembodied soul shall see;
> The pardon'd soul with solemn joy shall hail,
> When holiest rites are spent, and tears no more avail."
>
> —CARDINAL NEWMAN

POOR SOULS

ST. MICHAEL, GUARDIAN OF PURGATORY

There is a popular conception which connects St. Michael with the judgment of men. "He is shown with the Book of Life, or holding in his hands a pair of scales wherewith to weigh the souls of men. These are figurative expressions of the part popular devotion assigned to him in the great assize. It was this conception which inspired James Russell Lowell to write his poem, 'St. Michael the Weigher.' Standing in dazzling armor, the great Archangel is pictured by him uplifting the balance in his hand and weighing:

> "All man's dreaming, doing, saying,
> All the failure and the pain.
> All the triumph and the gain.

"Not merely is he now the protecting angel of a single people, nor even of all the faithful, but his office as here presented, would extend to all mankind. The idea is in a way suggested by the Church herself insofar as she refers to him as bringing souls from earth to the Throne of God. The priest prays at the Offertory of the Mass for the dead: 'May the standard bearer, St. Michael, lead them into the holy light.' But the poet sees him as the artist of the past had represented him, weighing all the thoughts and words and deeds of all mankind, since the day when Adam cast his last fond backward glance on the lost Paradise, and instead beheld the Cherubim and the inexorable blade of fire. And so, in stately words, the bard continues:

> "In a dream I marked him there,
> With his fire-gold flickering hair,
> In his blinding armor stand,
> And the scales were in his hand;
> Mighty were they, and full well
> They could poise both heaven and hell . . .
> In one scale I saw him place
> All the glories of our race,
> Cups that lit Belshazzar's feast,
> Gems the wonder of the East,
> Kublai's scepter, Caesar's sword,
> Many a poet's golden word,

"Many a skill of science vain
To make men as gods again.

In the other scale he threw
Things regardless, outcast, few,
Martyr-ash, arena-sand,
Of St. Francis' cord a strand,
Disillusions and despairs
Of young saints with grief-grayed hairs,
Broken hearts that break for man.

Marvel through my pulses ran
Seeing then the beam divine
Swiftly on this hand decline.
While earth's splendor and renown
Mounted light as thistle down.

"Such is the judgment of God as it differs from the judgment of men. So God's angels see and estimate our deeds." (Spirit World.)

In her beautiful prayers in the Mass of the dead, the Church with maternal solicitude places the souls of her departed children in the hands of St. Michael, that he may lead them into the kingdom of everlasting light. If St. Michael is so solicitous for the welfare of souls during their lifetime and at the hour of death, we may be certain that he will also befriend them during their stay in purgatory, and will hasten to bring them consolation. "Michael, my Archangel," sings the Church, "I have established thee Prince over all souls that are to be received into My Kingdom." "Bowing down with his hands joined and placed upon the altar shortly after the elevation, the Celebrant of the Mass says: 'We most humbly beseech Thee, Almighty God, to command these things to be carried by the hands of thy holy angel to the Altar on high, in the sight of Thy divine Majesty, that as many as shall partake of the most sacred Body and Blood of Thy Son at this altar may be filled with every heavenly grace and blessing.'

"It is estimated that there are thousands of Masses said daily and at every Mass there are angels present. Now, let us imitate the priest and invite these angels the world over to take all these chalices with the Sacred Blood from the altar and bring them to St. Michael, the guardian of Purgatory, that he may present this priceless treasure to the heavenly Father for the relief and release of the suffering souls. These then when liberated from their prison, will represent us in heaven to perform there the great work of loving, praising and glorifying the 'Lamb that was slain,' and to greet for us our heavenly Mother, who is in a particular manner the Queen of the holy souls in Purgatory. What a grand procession of angels with the Holy Grail hastening at our command from earth to Purgatory, to succor the poor souls, while our Redeemer is offering Himself on the altar! What acclamations of delight when this tide of Divine Blood overflows the earth and the refreshing flood reaches the flames of the truly banished children of Eve! What a grand array of purified souls leaving the land of woe and in company with their guardian angels flying to the realms of eternal bliss!" (Father Walz, C.PP.S.)

It is piously asserted that a Cistercian monk, after his death, appeared to one of his friends, a priest, and told him he would be delivered from Purgatory if during holy Mass the priest would invoke the intercession of St. Michael. The priest complied with this desire, and he, together with others who were present, had the consolation of seeing the soul of his friend taken up to heaven by the Archangel.

It is also related that a certain priest, whilst one day offering the Holy Sacrifice for the dead, recommended some souls in a particular manner by the words: "May the Prince of the angels, St. Michael, lead them into the glory of heaven." At the same instant he saw the glorious Archangel descend from heaven into Purgatory to deliver those souls and to conduct them into Paradise.

Let us be encouraged by these examples frequently to invoke the assistance of St. Michael in behalf of our departed loved ones and in particular to recommend them to his powerful intercession during the celebration of Holy Mass.

ST. MICHAEL, CHAMPION OF THE CHURCH

St. Michael has always been considered by the Church of God as its special Protector. Cardinal Newman hails him thus:

"Thou Champion high
Of Heaven's imperial Bride,
Forever waiting on her eye,
Before her onward path, and at her side,
In war her guard secure, by night her ready guide!"

Spiritual writers assure us that, "as the chosen people of the Old Law were marvelously protected by St. Michael, so we may not doubt that this great Prince of heaven protects the Church of God in a still more signal manner. Under the New Law as under the Old, St. Michael is the 'Vicar of the Most High and the Prince of His people,' ever prepared to render assistance. With one accord the holy Fathers of the Church teach that St. Michael is the Guardian Angel and the protector of the Catholic Church.

"Time and again, in centuries past, St. Michael came to the rescue when dreadful wars and persecutions threatened to destroy Christianity. He it was who, at the command of Mary, Queen of Angels, came to the assistance of Constantine the Great in the fourth century and helped his forces to gain a brilliant victory over the pagan Emperor Maxentius. The Archangel himself revealed his identity in this instance. Appearing to Constantine after the completion of a beautiful church which the latter had erected to his honor in gratitude, he said: I am Michael, the chief of the angelic legions of the Lord of hosts, the protector of the Christian religion, who whilst thou wast battling against godless tyrants, placed the weapons in thy hands.' This noble edifice, generally known as the Michaelion, became the scene of many miracles wrought through the power of the great Archangel.

"St. Michael has ever proved himself a valiant warrior for the honor of God both in heaven and on earth. By his power he wages incessant war with the archfiend, Satan, in the great kingdom of God upon earth, the Church. Glowing zeal for the honor of God in his distinctive trait and virtue.

"The Venerable Anna Catherine Emmerich was frequently granted visions of the past and future combats of the Church. Repeatedly she saw St. Michael, in the form of a warrior, standing with blood-stained sword above the Church, replacing the sword in his scabbard as a sign of victory. She was also shown how, in the present-day struggles of the Church, St. Michael would bring about a most glorious victory. This thought should be consoling to all the faithful Christians who view with alarm the many shafts of persecution now being directed against the Church." ('Neath St. Michael's Shield.) His assistance is needed by us, especially in these troublesome times when the legions of evil are almost visibly abroad over all the earth exciting the minds of men. We behold their activities, not merely in the world-wide Communist propaganda against morality and religion everywhere, but in other manifestations as well. Truly then, may we call on St. Michael to defend us in the tremendous day of battle, and to make strong our hearts that we may fight not merely a defensive warfare, but an aggressive spiritual campaign against evil under every shape. Beneath his mighty leadership and with the aid of his own unvanquishable legions of light, we shall not fail.

"Pope Leo XIII, realizing by divine enlightenment the present and future struggles of the Church against the powers of hell, felt convinced that through the intervention of St. Michael, hell would be conquered and the Church restored to peace and liberty. He, therefore, composed a prayer in honor of the warrior-Archangel and ordered it to be recited daily after low Mass in all the churches throughout the Christian world, which practice has been kept to this day. (This prayer will be found at the end of the book.) The circumstances which led to this course of action on the part of the saintly Pontiff are said to be as follows: One day, after having celebrated the holy Sacrifice of the Mass, the aged Pontiff was in conference with the Cardinals. Suddenly he sank to the floor in a deep swoon. Physicians who hastened to his side feared that he had already expired, for they could find no trace of his pulse. However, after a short interval the Holy Father rallied, and coming to himself, exclaimed with great emotion: 'Oh, what a horrible picture I have been permitted to see!' He had been shown in spirit the tremendous activities of the evil spirits and their efforts against the Church. But in the midst of this vision of horror he had beheld the consoling vision of the glorious Archangel Michael, who had appeared and cast Satan and his legions back into the abyss of hell. Soon afterwards he composed the well-known prayer: St. Michael, the Archangel defend us in the battle. Be our safeguard against the malice and snares of the devil . . ., etc. Daily this powerful petition rises heavenward from thousands of Catholic sanctuaries throughout the world and we may believe that in answer to this fervent plea the great Archangel hastens to the aid of the Bride of Christ, the Church, in her many afflictions."

Commenting on the grandeurs of our holy Mother the Church, Father Walz has this beautiful passage: "The Church of God has taken up her Bridegrooms' emblems of victory from Calvary's heights and has carried them throughout the world; for thus do I see the Church going forth over the earth, a valiant woman—in her left hand holding high the Cross and in her right devoutly carrying the Chalice, the two symbols of redemption, of truth and of grace. Her face is that of a victor who can speak of great triumphs, but the image of her Bridegroom, with whom she was espoused on the Cross, is ever reflected on her countenance . . . Beautiful as are the mysteries which she carries in her heart, they are contained in the Cross and in the Chalice of Blood, and by this is meant that all these mysteries have been bought at a great price, the price of the Precious Blood. 'He hath purchased the Church with His own Blood." (Acts XX, 28.)

As already mentioned, the Church has more than ever special need of the powerful protection of St. Michael in our perilous times. On all sides she is being assailed by strong and bitter enemies. In one country after another we behold the sad spectacle of religious persecution rising to an ever higher pitch of hatred and insolence. Surely the terrible crimes which have been committed in recent times and are still being committed against the Church, both in her sanctuaries and her members, are instigated by the devil, for no human mind could be base enough to conceive and put into execution such hideous outrages. The Church looks to St. Michael for aid that she may triumph over her persecutors and that the gates of hell may not prevail against her.

Assuredly, St. Michael will not fail to come to the aid of Holy Church in our days as he did in days of old, if we fervently and confidently implore him to do so. We know indeed that the gates of hell shall never prevail against the Church for Christ our Lord has promised to be with her till the end of time. Nevertheless, God wills that we do our part in defending her cause . . . He could confound the enemies of the Church by merely willing to do so. But He wills, rather, that we should co-operate in her defense, under the leadership of the great Captain of the heavenly hosts. Let us, therefore, most earnestly implore St. Michael to put an end to the persecutions which are assailing the Church in so many lands and to the activities of the evil spirits which are ruining so many souls." ('Neath St. Michael's Shield.)

"The Church visible is the monument of the Precious Blood against which the gates of hell shall not prevail. Let us then love the Church, the greatest gift of the Precious Blood, 'as Christ also loved the Church, and delivered Himself up for it . . . that He might present it to Himself a glorious Church, not having spot or wrinkle, or any such thing; but that it should be holy and without blemish'." (Eph. V, 25-27.)

THOU ART PETER . . . .

ST. MICHAEL AND THE FINAL TRIUMPH

And thou at last,
When time itself must die,
Shalt sound that dread and piercing blast,
To wake the dead, and rend the vaulted sky,
And summon all to meet the Omnipotent Judge on high.

—CARDINAL NEWMAN

Reference has already been made to the terrible struggle predicted for the last days. "We can realize the bitterness of the leader of the hosts of evil and the fierceness of the combats through which the Christians themselves will pass. Satan shall be loosed from prison, we are told. This is interpreted to mean that during the short time before the end there will be a lessening of that measure of restraint which had been placed upon him with the advent of Christ. 'And he shall come forth to lead astray the nations which are in the four corners of the earth.' (Apoc. XX, 7,8.) The number of his followers will be as the sands of the sea, and St. John beheld them in vision going up over the breadth of the earth and encompassing 'the camp of the saints and the beloved city.' Then it is that God's moment shall have arrived." (The Spirit World.)

The thought of the day of Judgment justly fills every thinking soul with a wholesome fear. "God has mercifully concealed from us the day and the hour when this dread event shall occur. Our Lord Himself after describing the terrors of the end of the world said to his diciples: 'But that day and hour no one knoweth, no, not even the angels in heaven, but the Father only.' (Matt. XXIV, 36.) Nevertheless, our Lord foretold certain signs which would precede the consummation of the world and which would serve as a warning to mankind of its approach. These signs are described in the Gospel of St. Mathews, as follows: 'For many will come in My Name, saying, I am the Christ,' and they will lead men astray. For you shall hear of wars and rumors of wars. Take care that you do not be alarmed, for these things must come to pass, but the end is not yet. For nation will rise against nation and kingdom against kingdom, and there will be pestilences and famines and earthquakes in various places . . . And then many will fall away and will betray one another and will hate one another. And many false prophets will arise, and shall lead many astray. And because iniquity will abound the charity of many will grow cold.' (Matt. XXIV, 5-7, 10-12.)

"Although we can see in our own times conditions such as are here described, this does not necessarily imply that the end of the world is near at hand. Nevertheless, we ought to take seriously to heart the critical condition of our present age and daily implore the mercy and the help of God. And since God Himself has appointed St. Michael as the special defender and advocate of the Christians against the Satanic powers, we ought to place ourselves with all confidence under his protection and daily invoke his aid for the Church and for immortal souls." ('Neath St. Michael's Shield.)

When the end of the world draws near, St. Michael will wage a final battle against the Antichrist, who by false miracles will endeavor to seduce even the elect of God. St. Michael will then defend the Church against frightful persecutions. In all quarters of the earth that last onset against the Church will break out under Satan's instigation. The entire struggle is summed up by St. John under one powerful picture in which we see the children of light making their brave and final stand for the Church of God and their Christian rights against the children of darkness who have been seduced by Satan. Then it is God's time to act and to end the role of Satan. He will be cast into hell forever.

After this most valiant Archangel has once more conquered the prince of darkness and has cast him into the abyss of hell, he will sound the dread trumpet whose resonance will call the dead to life and summon all men to appear before the Eternal Judge to receive their final sentence of reward or punishment. It is the General Judgment, and it is here that St. Michael will have to fulfill a ministry of awful import in the name of the Sovereign Judge. He with the rest of the angels will have to separate the good from the bad, all of whom will then have resumed their bodies in the general resurrection. It will be their duty to separate the cockle from the wheat; the wicked they shall cast into the furnace of fire, but the just shall 'shine as the sun in the Kingdom of their Father.'"

"The day of Judgment," writes Father Walz, "will see the rich harvest of the Blood of Calvary. Our Saviour will appear with His radiant Five Wounds, and the bodies of the just will reflect the glory of their Redeemer. The transfiguring of all glorified bodies into the likeness of the Body of Jesus is due to the merits of the Precious Blood. Oh, what honor, what glory, what ecstacy of joy to belong to that interminable array, that countless phalanx of the patriarchs and prophets, apostles and martyrs, virgins and confessors, of holy souls and glorified bodies, after the final Judgment leaving this earth forever, the place of their trials and struggles, singing songs of praise and following Our Lord and His Blessed Mother and the angels into everlasting happiness! St. John saw this final triumph of the Precious Blood when he wrote: 'Thou hast redeemed us, O Lord, in Thy Blood out of every tribe and tongue and people and nation, and Thou hast made us to become a kingdom unto our God'." (Apoc. V. 9.)

Happy shall we be if in that final hour we find an advocate in the glorious Archangel Michael! If we would insure for ourselves the intercession of this powerful champion before the Judgment seat of God, let us be faithful in invoking him often during life. Then will he be able to speak in our behalf these consoling words: "These are they who are come out of great tribulation, and have washed their robes and have made them white in the Blood of the Lamb." (Apoc. VII, 14.)

FEAST OF ST. MICHAEL

"Prince of the host of the Lord;
Standard Bearer;
Mighty Seraph;
One of the Seven that stand before the Throne;
Dauntless Challenger whose cry ran through the vasts
of heaven: 'Who is like to God!'

Guardian of God's chosen race,
Glorious Champion of the Church of Christ
under the New Law;
Triumphant Defender of the Woman and her Child;
Vanquisher of the Dragon and Chainer of his strength;
Leader of souls into the holy light."

—FATHER HUSSLEIN, S.J.

The above beautiful epigraph summarizes a few of the glorious prerogatives of the great Archangel whose feast the Church celebrates today under the title of: "Dedication of St. Michael." Her Liturgy is replete with the praises of St. Michael as the Prince of the heavenly hosts and as the protector of the children of God, and she sings the fulness of today's mystery, "For this is the day of Michael's most glorious feast which gladdens the whole earth with joy."

So let us rejoice with heaven and earth and congratulate St. Michael, Prince of the celestial army, on the splendor and glory that are his. We read in the Lives of the Saints, that this festival has been kept with great solemnity at the end of the month of September since at least the sixth century. Though only St. Michael is mentioned in the title, it appears from the prayers of the Mass, that all the good angels are its object, together with the glorious Prince and tutelary angel of the Church. On it we are called in a particular manner to give thanks to God for the glory which the angels enjoy and to rejoice in their happiness. Also to thank Him for His mercy to us in constituting such beings to minister to our salvation by aiding us . . . Lastly we are invited to honor them and implore their intercession and succor.

"As it is not certain just which church is commemorated as having been dedicated on this day, the pious belief has gained favor that the entire Catholic Church is here indicated. For, by casting the rebel spirits into the abyss. St. Michael dedicated the Church Triumphant in heaven as the peaceful abode of the angels, and as he wards off the devil and his colleagues from the Church upon earth, he has dedicated the Church Miltant as the secure dwelling place of the faithful upon earth. And we know how he succors the Church Suffering in Purgatory. This feast of St. Michael has ever been one of the outstanding feasts of the Church." ('Neath St. Michael's Shield.)

We have seen from the preceding pages how St. Michael has been venerated from earliest times. It is also interesting and consoling to note that the devotion has not diminished with the passing years. The Irish people have always held and still hold the Captain of the heavenly hosts in great veneration, as is evident from the number of ancient churches dedicated to him and the frequency with which his name is given even now to their children. They termed him "The high King of Angels." In England, veneration of St. Michael was at one time practiced so extensively that in the year 1114, King Ethelred ordained that the three days immediately preceding the feast of St. Michael should be days of strict fast. In the Middle Ages, the knights especially, consecrated themselves to St. Michael. The German people, too, have long been fervently devoted to this holy Archangel. And we have already mentioned how St. Joan of Arc, the liberator of France, ascribed her vocation and her victories to St. Michael. Three times he appeared to her in heavenly beauty and informed her that she was called to deliver her country. And so going through the records of time, it would seem that almost every nation, as well as every individual owes an immense debt of gratitude to the Marshal of Paradise. Devotion to St. Michael is likewise gaining favor in our own country, as is evidenced by the growing number of his clients.

Let us then heed this benevolent invitation and place great confidence in St. Michael. May we honor his feast day in a particular way by choosing him anew for our patron, that under his powerful leadership we may successfully attain eternal bliss. O glorious St. Michael, I believe in thy power and thy devotedness and put my trust in thee. Thou helpest all those who implore thee; obtain for me the grace of a tender devotion to thee, a devotion that will induce me often to invoke thee and hope from thee victory over temptations during life, special succor at the hour of death, particular protection at the divine Tribunal and prompt release from Purgatory. "Most glorious Prince, Archangel Michael, be mindful of us, pray here and everywhere always for us, the Son of God."

Yes, if we are faithful to him, he will not fail in his assistance towards us and how happy we shall be to meet at last this exalted Prince of the heavenly court and forever sing with him the praises of the "Lamb that was slain." For our presence in the heavenly Kingdom will be another conquest and an additional triumph of the redeeming Blood. "Thou hast redeemed us, O Lord God, in Thy Blood." This is the burden of the songs of the elect in heaven and they have become 'kings,' because they have conquered the world and hell, or the kingdom of Satan 'and they overcame him by the Blood of the Lamb' (Apoc. XII, 1); and they refer all the glory of heaven to the merits of the Blood of the Lamb. Glory to the Blood of Jesus now and forever and throughout all ages, for It was not shed in vain!" Thus will angels and men bear witness to the infinite mercies of the Blood of Christ.

> "Grant us with Michael still, O Lord,
> Against the prince of pride to fight;
> So may a crown be our reward,
> Before the Lamb's pure throne of light."

ASSUMPTION OF THE BLESSED VIRGIN INTO HEAVEN

MARY, QUEEN OF ANGELS

Bright angels are around thee,
They that have served thee from thy birth are there:
Their hands with stars have crowned thee;
Thou, —— peerless Queen of air,
As sandals to thy feet the silver moon dost wear.

—LUIS PONCE DE LEON
(Trans. by Henry W. Longfellow)

THIRTIETH DAY

MARY, QUEEN OF ANGELS

Sing, sing, ye Angel Bands,
All beautiful and bright;
For higher still and higher,
Through fields of starry light,
Mary, your Queen ascends,
Like the sweet moon at night.

A fairer flower than she
On earth hath never been;
And, save the Throne of God,
Your heavens have never seen
A wonder half so bright
As your ascending Queen!

And shall I loose thee then,
Loose my sweet right to thee?
Ah! no — the angel's Queen
Man's Mother still will be,
And thou upon thy throne,
Wilt keep thy love for me.

—FATHER FABER

It seems but fitting that we should close this lovely month of the angels by paying reverent and loving homage to her who is raised above all the angel choirs, Mary, their Queen.

It is the delight of these bright spirits to sing the praises of the Mother of God. Even the Seraphim have not a glory that in any way approaches hers. After her Incarnate Son, she is the splendor of the Heavenly Court, and the angels behold her in all her glory and are ravished at the sight. Is she not the Mother of their King and God? But what is it that exalts Mary above all the angels? Not merely her obedience to God, for this has always characterized them all, but rather her obedience in circumstances the most trying, amid suffering the most intense. In her compassion she approached most nearly to the Passion of her Son. None save Him ever surpassed her in suffering. She was the Queen of Martyrs, and therefore is the Queen of Angels. Thus it is that she has earned a more excellent reward than they.

The pious Boudon thus comments on her title, "Queen of Angels": "The Mother of God is the general of the armies of God and the angels form the glorious troops; thus they are the soldiers of her, who alone is terrible as a whole army in battle array, and in the beginning they fought valiantly for her honor in opposition to Lucifer and the apostate angels, who would not submit themselves to her empire, God having revealed to them that she should one day be their sovereign. She is the august and triumphant Queen of Paradise; the angels are those faithful and generous subjects who honored her as we have just now said, before she was, and who glory in being subject to the laws of her kingdom. She is the Lady of the Angels and is often invoked under this title of Our Lady of the Angels; they are then, her servants, but such zealous servants that they await but the manifestation of her will to execute it, at its least sign, with a promptitude that is indescribable. She is even their friend . . . and we may say, moreover, that she is in some manner their Mother and such is the opinion of many learned theologians. All these titles sufficiently show that the glory of this Queen, of this great and powerful Lady, is implied in the consideration shown to her subjects, her soldiers and her servants. The love which she bears them, treating them as her faithful friends and even as her children, calls upon us for every possible reason to love what she loves and to entertain the profoundest regard for those whom she desires to be honored. Let us then praise and bless the holy angels, because the most pure Virgin, the august Queen and Lady of the Angels, is praised and blessed by them."

But above all let us praise the Most High who through the Precious Blood has worked such wonders in our Lady and her clients. It is indeed to that Divine Blood that we owe our privileges and happiness. "The Precious Blood," says Father Walz, "is the fountain of the plenitude of all graces in Mary, but it is also the source of her power to help us. By her union with the Incarnate Word and by offering the Precious Blood in the temple and beneath the cross in union with her Divine Son, she became the Mother of the Saviour and the Mother of those who wish to be saved in His Sacred Blood. O my heavenly Queen, how could I ever forget thee? How could I but love thee? Forever and ever thou shalt be to me 'the Mother of fair love, and of fear, and of knowledge, and of holy hope.' The Precious Blood of thy Son shall ever remind me that it was taken from thy blood; just as my devotion to thee shall ever increase by devotion to the Price of my Redemption."

O Mother thou dist give to Christ
The Blood that made us free,
Sweet Fountain of the Precious Blood
We place our trust in thee.

While being the song of angels, the Sacred Blood "was the light of Mary's darkness and the jubilee of all her woes," adds Father Faber. "It turned her sufferings into dignities and crowns. Her holiness which enchants all heaven, is the monument and trophy of that victorious Blood."

Sweet Lady of the Angels, dearest Mother of men, be mindful of thy children of earth, lonely "Pilgrims of the Night." Be thou with us throughout life's journey, and at eventide, be thou near with thine angels to comfort and welcome us to our heavenly Father's home. Meanwhile, may our mortal ears become more attuned to Angelic strains inviting us to rise ever higher above the earth earthly, in the ways of divine love and light.

"Angels! sing on, your faithful watches keeping,
Sing us sweet fragments of the songs above;
While we toil on, and soothe ourselves with weeping,
Till life's long night shall break in endless love.

Angels of Jesus,
Angels of light,
Singing to welcome
The pilgrims of the night!"

—FATHER FABER

As a parting tribute of filial love to our sweet Mother in heaven, Our Lady of the Angels, may we make our own these tender, prayerful lines of the saintly Cardinal Wiseman:

"The Lord is with thee! My Mother dear,
Thou art never weary that news to hear—
The gladdest news that was ever told,
Forever new and forever old,

"Thy children are telling it all day long,
And the angels make it their sweetest song;
And we hail thee, and bless thee, and love to tell
He's ever with thee—the Mother He loves so well.

"He came to thee first in the midnight gloom
That wrapped thee round in the silent room,
When the listening air was thrilled and stirred
By the breath of Gabriel's wondrous word—

And the silver wings of the Heavenly Dove,
Drooped, brooding o'er His Virgin Love,
And thy Jesus came to thy heart unseen
As the angel knelt to the angels' Queen.

He came to thee first—He is with thee now,
He has set a crown on thy shining brow,
He is with thee forever—no more to part,
For thy home of love is His Sacred Heart.
Hail Mary! my Mother, thy joy is won,
The Lord is with thee! thy Lord and Son;
Hail Mary! my Mother! thy pains are past,
And forever and ever thy bliss shall last.

Hail Mary! Again and again we greet
The Mother of God and our Mother sweet,
We look on that beautiful, loving face
So full of glory, so full of grace,
And we sigh for the day when we shall rest·
In thy tender arms, on thy loving breast,
The day when our exile will be past
When thou shalt show us thy Child at last.

O Mary! to think we shall see thee then,
The face we have dreamed of again and again,
To think—oh, can it ever be true
That the Lord will be with us too?
That through all those bright, unending hours,
Jesus and Mary will both be ours.

PRAYER TO THE QUEEN OF ANGELS

(by St. Frances of Rome)

Hail Daughter and Handmaid of the Most High King and
Spouse of the Holy Ghost; we beseech thee that thou, with St.
Michael the Archangel, and all the Powers of heaven, and all the
saints, wouldst deign to intercede for us with thy most beloved
Son, our Lord and Master, Who with the same Father and Holy
Ghost, liveth and reigneth forever and ever. Amen.

PRAYERS

IN HONOR OF

ST. MICHAEL

AND

THE HOLY ANGELS

THE HOLY TRINITY

How wonderful is life in heaven
Amid the angelic choirs,
Where uncreated Love has crowned
His first created fires!

And oh, how lovely they must be
Whom God has glorified;
Yet one of them, oh sweetest thought,
Is ever at my side.

—FATHER FABER

MASS FOR THE DEDICATION OF ST. MICHAEL

(September 29th)

INTROIT. Ps. 102. Bless the Lord all ye His angels: you that are mighty in strength, and execute His words, hearkening to the voice of His orders. Ps. Bless the Lord, O my soul; and let all that is within me bless His holy Name. V. Glory be to the Father . . .

COLLECT. O God, who, in a wonderful order, providest ministries both of angels and of men; grant in Thy mercy, that they who ever stand before Thy face to minister unto Thee in heaven may protect us during our life upon earth. Through Our Lord.

LESSON FROM THE APOCALYPSE, C. 1. In those days God signified the things which must shortly come to pass, and He sent and signified them through His angel to His servant John, who bore witness to the word of God, and to the testimony of Jesus Christ, to whatever he saw. Blessed is he who reads and those who hear the words of this prophecy, and keep the things that are written therein; for the time is at hand. John to the seven churches that are in Asia: Grace be to you and peace from Him who is, and who was and who is coming, and from the seven spirits who are before His throne; and from Jesus Christ who is the faithful witness, the first born of the dead, and the ruler of the kings of the earth. To Him who has loved us and washed us from our sins in His own Blood.

GRADUAL. Bless the Lord, all you His angels: you that are mighty in strength, that do His will. Bless the Lord, O my soul: and all that is within me bless His holy Name. Alleluia, alleluia. Holy Archangel Michael, defend us in the battle: that we may not perish in the dreadful judgment. Alleluia.

(Instead of the above, the following is said during Easter time) ALLELUIA, ALLELUIA. Holy Archangel Michael, defend us in the battle, that we may not perish in the dreadful judgment. Alleluia. The sea was shaken and the earth trembled when the Archangel Michael came down from heaven. Alleluia.

GOSPEL. MATTHEW C. 18. At that time: the disciples came to Jesus saying: "Who then is the greatest in the kingdom of heaven?" and Jesus, calling a little child to Him, set it in the midst of them and said: "Amen I say to you, unless you be converted and become as little children, you shall not enter into the kingdom of heaven.

Whoever, therefore, humbles himself as this little child, he is the greatest in the kingdom of heaven: and whoever receives one such little child for My sake, receives Me. But whoever causes one of these little ones who believe in Me to sin, it were better for him to have a millstone hung around his neck, and to be drowned in the depths of the sea. Woe to the world because of scandals! For it must needs be that scandals come; but woe to the man through whom scandal does come. And if thy hand or thy foot is an occasion of sin to thee, cut it off and cast it from thee. It is better for thee to enter life maimed or lame, than having two hands or two feet, to be cast into everlasting fire. And if thy eye is an occasion of sin to thee, pluck it out and cast it from thee. It is better for thee to enter into life with one eye, than having two eyes, to be cast into the hell of fire. See that you do not despise one of these little ones; for I tell you, their angels in heaven always behold the Face of My Father who is in heaven."

OFFERTORY. APOC. 8.   An angel stood near the altar of the temple, having a golden censer in his hand; and there was given to him much incense; and the smoke of the perfumes ascended before God.

SECRET.   We offer Thee a sacrifice of praise, O Lord, and humbly beseech Thee that, through the prayers of Thy holy angels, who plead for us, Thou wouldst graciously receive it, and grant that it may avail us unto salvation. Through Our Lord . . .
COMMUNION. DAN. 3.   All ye angels of the Lord, bless the Lord: sing a hymn and exalt Him above all forever.

POSTCOMMUNION.   Supported by the intercession of blessed Michael Thine Archangel, we humbly entreat Thee, O Lord, that the service we pay with our lips, we may lay hold of with our minds. Through Our Lord.

HYMNS FROM THE OFFICE OF ST. MICHAEL

O Jesus! Life-spring of the soul!
The Father's power and glory bright!
Thee with the Angels we extol;
From Thee they draw their life and light.

Thy thousand, thousand hosts are spread
Embattled o'er the azure sky;
But Michael bears Thy standard dread
And lifts the mighty Cross on high.

He in that sign the rebel powers
Did with their dragon prince expel,
And hurled them from the heaven's high towers,
Down like a thunderbolt to hell.

Grant us with Michael still, O Lord,
Against the prince of pride to fight;
So may a crown be our reward,
Before the Lamb's pure throne of light.

To God the Father praise be done,
Who hath redeemed us through His Son;
Anoints us by the Holy Ghost,
And guards us by the angel-host. Amen.

O Christ, the glory of the Angel choirs!
Of man the Maker and Redeemer blest!
Grant us one day to reach those bright abodes,
And in Thy glory rest.

Angel of Peace! thou, Michael, from above,
Come down, amid the homes of man to dwell;
And banish wars with all their tears and blood,
Back to their native hell.

Angel of Strength! thou, Gabriel, cast out
Thine ancient foes, usurpers of thy reign;
The temples of thy thriumph round the globe,
Revisit once again.

And Raphael, physician of the soul—
Let him descend from his pure halls of light,
To heal our sicknesses, and guide for us
Each dubious course aright.

Thou, too, fair Virgin, Daughter of the skies!
Mother of light, and Queen of Peace! descend;
Bringing with thee the radiant court of heaven,
To aid us and defend.

This grace on us bestow, O Father blest!
And Thou, O Son by an eternal birth;
With Thee, from both proceeding, Holy Ghost,
Whose glory fills the earth. Amen.

PRAYER AFTER LOW MASS

(Promulgated by Pope Leo XIII)

St. Michael, the Archangel, defend us in the day of battle; be our safeguard against the wickedness and snares of the devil. May God rebuke him, we humbly pray: and do thou, Prince of the heavenly host, by the power of God thrust down to hell Satan and all the wicked spirits, who wander through the world seeking the ruin of souls. Amen.

PRAYER FOR THE CHURCH AND FOR SOULS

(Recommended for frequent recitation in the present critical times)

O glorious Archangel, St. Michael, Prince of the heavenly host, be our defense in the terrible warfare which we carry on against principalities and powers, against the rulers of this world of darkness, the spirits of evil. Come to the aid of man, whom God has created immortal, made in His own image and likeness, and redeemed at a great price from the tyranny of the devil. Fight this day the battle of the Lord, together with the holy angels, as already thou hast fought the leader of the proud angels, Lucifer, and his apostate host, who were powerless to resist thee, nor was there place for them longer in heaven.

That cruel, that ancient serpent, who is called the devil or Satan, who seduces the whole world, was cast into the abyss with his angels. Behold, this primeval enemy and slayer of men has taken courage. Transformed into an angel of light, he wanders about with all the multitude of wicked spirits, invading the earth in order to blot out the Name of God and of His Christ, to seize upon, slay and cast into eternal perdition the souls destined for the crown of eternal glory. This wicked dragon pours out, as a most impure flood, the venom of his malice on men of depraved mind and corrupt heart, the spirit of lying, of impiety, of blasphemy, and the pestilent breath of impurity, and of every vice and iniquity. These most crafty enemies have filled and inebriated with gall and bitterness the Church, the Spouse of the immaculate Lamb, and have laid impious hands on her most sacred possessions. In the Holy Place itself, where has been set up the See of the most holy Peter and the Chair of Truth for the light of the world, they have raised the throne of their abominable impiety, with the iniquitous design that when the pastor has been struck the sheep may be scattered.

Arise, then, O invincible Prince, bring help to the people of God against the attacks of the lost spirits, and give them the victory. They venerate thee as their protector and patron; in thee Holy Church glories as her defence against the malicious power of hell; to thee has God entrusted the souls of men to be established in heavenly beatitude. Oh, pray to the God of peace that He may put Satan under our feet, so far conquered that he may no longer be able to hold man in captivity and harm the Church. Offer our prayers in the sight of the Most High, so that they may quickly conciliate the mercies of the Lord; and beating down the dragon, the ancient serpent, who is the devil and Satan, do thou again make him captive in the abyss, that he may no longer seduce the nations. Amen.

V. Behold the Cross of the Lord; be scattered, ye hostile powers.
R. The Lion of the tribe of Juda has conquered, the root of David.

V. Let Thy mercies be upon us, O Lord.
R. As we have hoped in Thee.

V. O Lord, hear my prayer,
R. And let my cry come unto Thee.

Let us pray: O God, the Father of our Lord Jesus Christ, we call upon Thy holy Name, and as supplicants we implore Thy clemency, that by the intercession of Mary, ever Virgin Immaculate and our Mother, and of the glorious Archangel St. Michael, Thou wouldst deign to help us against Satan and all other unclean spirits, who wander about the world for the injury of the human race and the ruin of souls. Amen.

Saint Michael the Archangel, defend us in the battle, that we may not perish in the fearful judgment. (Roman Missal) (300 days ind., a plenary indulgence under the usual conditions, for the devout recitation of this invocation every day for a month.)

Saint Michael, first champion of the Kingship of Christ, pray for us. (300 days)

PRAYER FOR HELP AGAINST SPIRITUAL ENEMIES

Glorious St. Michael, Prince of the heavenly hosts, who standest always ready to give assistance to the people of God; who didst fight with the dragon, the old serpent, and didst cast him out of heaven, and now valiantly defendest the Church of God that the gates of hell may never prevail against her, I earnestly entreat thee to assist me also, in the painful and dangerous conflict which I have to sustain against the same formidable foe. Be with me, O mighty Prince! that I may courageously fight and wholly vanquish that proud spirit, whom thou hast by the Divine Power, so gloriously overthrown, and whom our powerful King, Jesus Christ, has, in our nature, so completely overcome; to the end that having triumphed over the enemy of my salvation, I may with thee and the holy angels, praise the clemency of God who, having refused mercy to the rebellious angels after their fall, has granted repentance and forgiveness to fallen man. Amen.

NOVENA IN HONOR OF ST. MICHAEL AND
ALL THE HOLY ANGELS

First Day. Ardent Seraphim, you who dwell in the eternal home of love, unceasingly absorbed in the rays of the Sun of Justice, we beg you in virtue of the Divine Blood, to enkindle in our hearts that holy fire with which you are consumed.

St. Michael, the Archangel, and all ye Holy Angels, protect us in our combats, that we may not perish in the tremendous judgment of God.

Glory be to the Father, and to the Son and to the Holy Ghost. As it was in the beginning, is now and ever shall be, world without end. Amen.

Second Day. Bright Cherubim, you who are allowed a deeper insight into God's secrets, dispel the darkness of our souls, and in virtue of the Divine Blood, give that supernatural light to our eyes that will enable us to understand the truths of salvation.

St. Michael, the Archangel, etc.
Glory be to the Father, etc.

Third Day. Sublime Thrones, dazzling in your beauty, upon whom rests the Almighty and who convey His commands to the inferior Angels, obtain for us in virtue of the Divine Blood, peace with God, with our neighbor and with ourselves.

St. Michael, the Archangel, etc.
Glory be to the Father, etc.

Fourth Day. Supreme Dominations, you who have authority over all the Angelic Choirs, and are charged with the execution of God's orders, rule over our minds and hearts, and in virtue of the Divine Blood, help us to know and faithfully to accomplish the will of God.

St. Michael, the Archangel, etc.
Glory be to the Father, etc.

Fifth Day. Invincible Powers, whose mission it is to remove the obstacles to the Divine will, and to overcome its enemies, defend us against the attacks of the world, the flesh and the devil, and in virtue of the Divine Blood, render us victorious in our combats against this triple power.

St. Michael, the Archangel, etc.
Glory be to the Father, etc.

Sixth Day. Heavenly Virtues, who watch over the harmony of the material creation, you whose name signifies "Strength," have pity on our weakness, and obtain for us in virtue of the Divine Blood, the grace to bear with patience the trials of this life.

St. Michael, the Archangel, etc.
Glory be to the Father, etc.

Seventh Day. Sovereign Principalities, you who are the Princes of Nations, we beseech you to guard our Country effectively, that it may realize God's designs in its regard. Govern also our souls and our bodies, and in virtue of the Divine Blood, obtain that we may attain eternal life.

St. Michael, the Archangel, etc.
Glory be to the Father, etc.

Eighth Day. Most noble Archangels, you who, under the command of St. Michael, guard and protect the Holy Church, deign to deliver her from internal and external enemies. Watch over the Holy Father, as well as over all the children of the Immaculate Spouse of Christ, and in virtue of the Divine Blood, obtain for us the grace to live and die in the Faith, Hope and Charity of Holy Church, so that we may be eternally united with its august Head, Jesus Christ, Our Lord.

St. Michael, the Archangel, etc.
Glory be to the Father, etc.

Ninth Day. Most holy Angels, you whose zeal for the interests of God, wherever they need to be defended, carries your through the universe more rapidly than lightning, protect His cause in our souls, and in virtue of the Divine Blood, obtain for us the signal grace of final perseverance.

St. Michael, the Archangel, etc.
Glory be to the Father, etc.

Antiphon: O most glorious Prince, Michael, the Archangel, be mindful of us, here and everywhere, and always pray to the Son of God for us.

Verse: I will praise Thee, O God, in the sight of Thy Angels.

Response: I will adore Thee in Thy holy Temple and I will confess Thy Name.

LET US PRAY

O God, Who hast in an admirable order disposed the ministry of angels and of men, grant in Thy goodness that our life on earth may be protected by those who in heaven always assist before Thy throne ready to do Thy will. Through Our Lord, Jesus Christ. Amen.

(A novena may be made at any time of the year, with any form of approved prayers. Many of the prayers given here may be used for this purpose. By this exercise, the faithful may gain an indulgence of five years on each day, and a plenary indulgence at the end of their novena under the usual conditions.) ("Preces et Pia Opera," 409.)

PRAYER TO ST. MICHAEL

Glorious Prince of the heavenly hosts and victor over rebellious spirits, be mindful of me who am so weak and sinful and yet so prone to pride and ambition. Lend me, I pray, thy powerful aid in every temptation and difficulty, and above all do not forsake me in my last struggle with the powers of evil. Amen.

PRAYER FOR PROTECTION OF THE CHURCH AND HER MEMBERS

O glorious St. Michael, guardian and defender of the Church of Jesus Christ, come to the assistance of this Church, against which the powers of hell are unchained, guard with especial care her august Head, and obtain that for him and for us the hour of triumph may speedily arrive. O glorious Archangel St. Michael, watch over us during life, defend us against the assaults of the demon, assist us especially at the hour of death; obtain for us a favorable judgment, and the happiness of beholding God face to face for endless ages. Amen.

LITANY OF ST. MICHAEL

(For private use)

Lord, have mercy on us.
Christ, have mercy on us.
Lord, have mercy on us.
Christ, hear us.
Christ, graciously hear us.
God the Father of heaven, have mercy on us.
God the Son, redeemer of the world, have mercy on us.
God the Holy Ghost, have mercy on us.
Holy Trinity, one God, have mercy on us.
Holy Mary, Queen of Angels,
St. Michael,
St. Michael, filled with the wisdom of God,
St. Michael, perfect adorer of the Incarnate Word,
St. Michael, crowned with honor and glory,
St. Michael, most powerful Prince of the armies of the Lord,
St. Michael, standard-bearer of the Most Holy Trinity,
St. Michael, guardian of Paradise,
St. Michael, guide and comforter of the people of Israel,

Pray for Us

109

St. Michael, splendor and fortress of the Church Militant,
St. Michael, honor and joy of the Church Triumphant,
St. Michael, light of angels,
St. Michael, bulwark of orthodox believers,
St. Michael, strength of those who fight under the standard of the Cross,
St. Michael, light and confidence of souls at the hour of death,
St. Michael, our most sure aid,
St. Michael, our help in all adversities,
St. Michael, herald of the everlasting sentence,
St. Michael, consoler of souls detained in the flames of purgatory,
Thou, whom the Lord hath charged to receive souls after death,
St. Michael, our Prince,
St. Michael, our Advocate,

Pray for Us

Lamb of God, who takest away the sins of the world, spare us, O Lord.
Lamb of God, who takest away the sins of the world, graciously hear us, O Lord.
Lamb of God, who takest away the sins of the world, have mercy on us.
Christ hear us.
Christ graciously hear us.
V.   Pray for us, O glorious St. Michael, Prince of the Church of Jesus Christ.
R.   That we may be made worthy of His promises.

Let Us Pray: Sanctify us, we beseech Thee, O Lord, with Thy holy blessing, and grant us, by the intercession of St. Michael, that wisdom which teaches us to lay up treasures in heaven by exchanging the goods of this world for those of eternity, Thou who livest and reignest world without end. Amen.

PRAYER TO ST. MICHAEL ARCHANGEL

St. Michael, the Archangel! Glorious Prince, chief and champion of the heavenly hosts; guardian of the souls of men; conqueror of the rebel angels! How beautiful art thou, in thy heaven-made armour. We love thee, dear Prince of Heaven!

We, thy happy clients, yearn to enjoy thy special protection. Obtain for us from God a share of thy sturdy courage; pray that we may have a strong and tender love for our Redeemer and, in every danger or temptation, be invincible against the enemy of our souls. O standard-bearer of our salvation! Be with us in our last moments and when our souls quit this earthly exile, carry them safely to the judgment seat of Christ, and may Our Lord and Master bid thee bear us speedily to the kingdom of eternal bliss. Teach us ever to repeat thy sublime cry: "Who is like unto God?" Amen.

MASS FOR THE FEAST OF ST. GABRIEL ARCHANGEL

(March 24)

INTROIT. Ps. cii. 20.   Bless the Lord, all ye His Angels; you that are mighty in strength, and execute His word, hearkening to the voice of His orders. Ps. Bless the Lord, O my soul: and let all that is within me bless His holy Name. Glory be to the Father, etc.

COLLECT.   O God who didst choose from among all other angels the Archangel Gabriel to announce the mystery of Thine Incarnation, grant in Thy mercy that celebrating his feast on earth, we may reap the effect of his protection in heaven. Who livest . . .

EPISTLE. Daniel ix. 21-26.   Lesson from the Prophet Daniel. In those days behold the man Gabriel, whom I had seen in the vision at the beginning, flying swiftly, touched me at the time of the evening sacrifice. And he instructed me and spoke to me and said: O Daniel, I am now come forth to teach thee, that thou mightest understand. From the beginning of thy prayers the word came forth: and I am come to show it to thee, because thou art a man of desires. Therefore, do thou mark the word and understand the vision. Seventy weeks are shortened upon thy people and upon thy holy city, that transgression may be finished and sin may have an end and iniquity may be abolished, and everlasting justice may be brought and vision and prophecy may be fulfilled and the Saint of saints may be anointed. Know thou therefore, and take notice: that from the going forth of the world to build up Jerusalem again, unto Christ the Prince, there shall be seven weeks and sixty-two weeks: and the street shall be built again, and the walls in staitness of times. And after sixty-two weeks Christ shall be slain: and the people that shall deny Him shall not be His. And a people with their leader that shall come, shall destroy the city and the sanctuary; and the end thereof shall be waste, and after the end of the war the appointed desolation.

GRADUAL. Ps. cii. 20, 1.   Bless the Lord, all ye His angels, you that are mighty in strength and execute His words. Bless the Lord, O my soul, and let all that is within me bless His holy Name.

GOSPEL. Luke i 26-38.   Continuation of the holy Gospel according to St. Luke. In those days the angel Gabriel was sent from God into a city of Galilee, called Nazareth, to a virgin espoused to a man whose name was Joseph, of the house of David: and the virgin's name was Mary. And the angel being come in, said unto her: Hail, full of grace, the Lord is with thee; blessed are thou among women. Who having heard, was troubled at his saying and thought with herself what manner of salutation this should be. And the angel said to her: Fear not Mary, for thou hast found grace with God. Behold thou shalt conceive in thy womb and shall bring forth a son: and thou shalt call His name Jesus. He shall be great and shall be called the Son of the Most High. And the Lord God shall give unto Him the throne of David His father: and He shall reign in the house of Jacob forever. And of His kingdom there shall be no end. And Mary said to the angel: How shall this be done, because I know not man? And the angel answering, said to her: The Holy Ghost shall come upon thee and the power of the Most High shall overshadow thee. And therefore also the Holy which shall be born of thee shall be called the Son of God. And behold thy cousin Elizabeth, she also hath conceived a son in her old age: and this is the sixth month with her that is called barren: because no word shall be impossible with God. And Mary said: Behold the handmaid of the Lord; be it done to me according to Thy word.

OFFERTORY. APOC. viii. 3, 4.   An angel stood near the altar of the temple, having a golden censer in his hand and there was given to him much incense and the smoke of the perfume ascended before God.

SECRET.   May the offering of our service and the prayer of the blessed Archangel Gabriel be acceptable in Thy sight, O Lord; that he whom we venerate on earth, may be our advocate before Thee in heaven. Through our Lord.

COMMUNION. Daniel iii. 58.   All ye angels of the Lord, bless the Lord: sing a hymn, and exalt Him above all for ever.

POSTCOMMUNION.   Having partaken in the mysteries of Thy Body and Blood, we implore Thy clemency, O Lord our God; that we to whom Thine Incarnation was made known by the message of Gabriel, may likewise obtain through His help the benefits of that same Incarnation. Who livest, etc.

HYMNS FROM THE OFFICE OF ST. GABRIEL

O Christ, the glory of the Angel choirs!
Of man the Maker and Redeemer blest!
Grant us one day to reach those bright abodes,
And in Thy glory rest.

Angel of Strength! thou, Gabriel, cast out
Thine ancient foes, usurpers of thy reign;
The temples of thy triumph round the globe,
Revisit once again.

Thou, too, fair Virgin, Daughter of the skies!
Mother of light and Queen of Peace! descend;
Bringing with thee the radiant court of heaven,
To aid us and defend.

This grace on us bestow, O Father blest!
And Thou, O Son by an eternal birth;
With Thee, from both proceeding, Holy Ghost,
Whose glory fills the earth. Amen.

O Christ, Thy guilty people spare!
Lo, bending at Thy gracious throne,
Thy Virgin Mother pours her prayer,
Imploring pardon for her own.

Be near us, Angel from the skies,
Whose name Strength of God signifies;
All ills of flesh take thou away,
Bring health to souls from truth that stray.

Ye Angels, happy evermore!
Who in your circles nine ascend,
As ye have guarded us before,
So still from harm our steps defend.

Drive from the flock, O Spirits blest!
The false and faithless race away;
That all within one fold may rest,
Secure beneath one Shepherd's sway.

To God the Father glory be,
And to His sole-begotten Son;
The same, O Holy Ghost, to thee,
While everlasting ages run. Amen.

PRAYER TO ST. GABRIEL ARCHANGEL

O Blessed Archangel Gabriel, we beseech thee, do thou intercede for us at the throne of divine Mercy in our present necessities, that as thou didst announce to Mary the mystery of the Incarnation, so through thy prayers and patronage in heaven we may obtain the benefits of the same, and sing the praise of God forever in the land of the living. Amen.

PRAYER TO ST. GABRIEL ARCHANGEL

O loving messenger of the Incarnation, descend upon all those for whom I wish peace and happiness. Spread your wings over the cradles of the new-born babes, O thou who didst announce the coming of the Infant Jesus.

Give to the young a lily petal from the virginal sceptre in your hand. Cause the Ave Maria to re-echo in all hearts that they may find grace and joy through Mary.

Finally, recall the sublime words spoken on the day of the Annunciation—"Nothing is impossible with God," and repeat them in hours of trial—to all those I love—that their confidence in Our Lord may be reanimated, when all human help fails. Amen.

PRAYER OF THE CHURCH

May the offering of our service and the prayer of the blessed Archangel Gabriel be acceptable in Thy sight, O Lord; that he whom we venerate on earth, may be our advocate before Thee in heaven. Through Our Lord. Amen. (Secret of the Mass for the feast of St. Gabriel Archangel.)

PRAYER TO THE HOLY ARCHANGEL WHO STRENGTHENED OUR LORD IN HIS AGONY

(Believed by some to be St. Gabriel)

O holy Angel who didst strengthen Jesus Christ our Lord, come and strengthen us also; come and tarry not! (300 days indulgence. "Preces et Pia Opera," 417.)

I salute thee, holy Angel who didst comfort my Jesus in His agony, and with thee I praise the most holy Trinity for having chosen thee from among all the holy Angels to comfort and strengthen Him who is the comfort and strength of all that are in affliction. By the honor thou didst enjoy and by the obedience, humility and love wherewith thou didst assist the sacred Humanity of Jesus, my Saviour, when He was fainting for very sorrow at seeing the sins of the world and especially my sins, I beseech thee to obtain for me perfect sorrow for my sins; deign to strengthen me in the afflictions that now overwhelm me, and in all the other trials, to which I shall be exposed henceforth and, in particular, when I find myself in my final agony. Amen. (500 days indulgence. "Preces et Pia Opera," 418.)

LITANY OF ST. GABRIEL

(for private use)

Lord, have mercy on us,
Christ, have mercy on us,
Lord, have mercy on us,
Christ, hear us,
Christ, graciously hear us,
God the Father of heaven, have mercy on us,
God the Son, Redeemer of the world, have mercy on us,
God the Holy Ghost, have mercy on us,
Holy Trinity, one God, have mercy on us,

Holy Mary, Queen of Angels,*
Saint Gabriel, glorious Archangel,
St. Gabriel, Strength of God,
St. Gabriel, who standest before the throne of God,
St. Gabriel, model of prayer,
St. Gabriel, Herald of the Incarnation,
St. Gabriel, who didst reveal the glories of Mary,
St. Gabriel, Prince of heaven,
St. Gabriel, Ambassador of the Most High,
St. Gabriel, Guardian of the Immaculate Virgin,
St. Gabriel, who didst foretell the greatness of Jesus,
St. Gabriel, peace and light of souls,
St. Gabriel, scourge of unbelievers,
St. Gabriel, admirable teacher,
St. Gabriel, strength of the just,
St. Gabriel, protector of the faithful,
St. Gabriel, first adorer of the Divine Word,
St. Gabriel, defender of the faith,
St. Gabriel, zealous for the honor of Jesus Christ,
St. Gabriel, whom the Scriptures praise as the Angel sent by
       God to Mary, the Virgin,

Pray for Us

Lamb of God who takest away the sins of the world, spare us, O Lord,

Lamb of God who takest away the sins of the world, graciously hear us, O Lord,

Lamb of God who takest away the sins of the world, have mercy on us.

Christ, hear us,

Christ, graciously hear us.

V. Pray for us, blessed Archangel Gabriel.

R. That we may be made worthy of the promises of Jesus Christ.

Let us pray: O blessed Archangel Gabriel, we beseech thee, do thou intercede for us at the throne of divine Mercy in our present necessities, that as thou didst announce to Mary the mystery of the Incarnation, so through thy prayers and patronage in heaven, we may obtain the benefits of the same, and sing the praise of God forever in the land of the living. Amen.

MASS FOR THE FEAST OF ST. RAPHAEL ARCHANGEL

(October 24)

INTROIT. Ps. cii. 20. Bless the Lord, all ye His angels; you that are mighty in strength and execute His word, hearkening to the voice of His orders. Ps. Bless the Lord, O my soul, and let all that is within me bless His holy name. Glory be to the Father, etc.

COLLECT. O God who to Tobias, Thy servant, when on his journey, didst give blessed Raphael the Archangel, as a companion; grant to us Thy servants, that we may be ever protected by his custody and strengthened by his help. Through Our Lord . . .

EPISTLE. Tobias xii. 7-15. Lesson from the Book of Tobias. In those days, the angel Raphael said to Tobias: It is good to hide the secret of a king: but honourable to reveal and confess the works of God. Prayer is good with fasting and alms, more than to lay up treasures of gold: for alms delivereth from death, and the same is that which purgeth away sins, and maketh to find mercy and life everlasting. But they that commit sin and iniquity are enemies to their own soul. I discover then the truth unto you, and I will not hide the secret from you. When thou didst pray with tears, and didst bury the dead, and didst leave thy dinner, and hide the dead by day in thy house, and bury them by night, I offered thy prayer to the Lord. And because thou wast acceptable to God, it was necessary that temptation should prove thee. And now the Lord hath sent me to heal thee, and to deliver Sara thy son's wife from the devil. For I am the angel Raphael, one of the seven who stand before the Lord.

GRADUAL. Tobias viii. 3. The angel of the Lord, Raphael, took and bound the devil. V. Great is our Lord, and great is His power.

Alleluia, alleluia. V. I will sign praise to thee in the sight of the angels, I will worship towards Thy holy temple, and I will give glory to Thy name, O Lord. Alleluia.

GOSPEL. John v. 1-15. Continuation of the Holy Gospel according to St. John. At that time there was a festival day of the Jews, and Jesus went up to Jerusalem. Now there is at Jerusalem a pond called Probatica, which in Hebrew is named Bethsaida, having five porches. In these lay a great multitude of sick, of blind, of lame, of withered, waiting for the moving of the water. And an angel of the Lord descended at certain times into the pond, and the water was moved. And he that went down first into the pond after the motion of the water was made whole of whatsoever infirmity he lay under.

OFFERTORY. Apoc. viii. 3, 4. An angel stood near the altar of the temple, having a golden censer in his hand, and there was given to him much incense, and the smoke of the perfumes ascended before God.

SECRET. We offer Thee, O Lord, the sacrifice of praise, most humbly beseeching Thee, that Thy holy angels pleading for us, Thou wouldst graciously receive it and make it to avail to our salvation. Through Our Lord.

COMMUNION. All ye angels of the Lord, bless the Lord: sing a hymn, and exalt Him above all for ever.

POSTCOMMUNION. Vouchsafe, O Lord our God, to send Thy holy Archangel Raphael to our aid; and may he, whom we faithfully believe ever to stand before Thy Majesty, present our humble prayers to Thee for Thy blessing. Through our Lord.

HYMNS FROM THE OFFICE OF ST. RAPHAEL

O Christ, the glory of the Angel choirs!
Of man the Maker and Redeemer blest!
Grant us one day to reach those bright abodes,
And in Thy glory rest.

And Raphael, physician of the soul,
Let him descend from his pure halls of light,
To heal our sicknesses and guide for us
Each dubious course aright.

Thou, too, fair Virgin, Daughter of the skies!
Mother of light and Queen of Peace! descend;
Bringing with thee the radiant court of heaven
To aid us and defend.

This grace on us bestow, O Father blest,
And Thou, O Son by an eternal birth;
With thee, from both proceeding, Holy Ghost,
Whose glory fills the earth. Amen.

O Christ, thy servants' wanderings spare;
For whom Thy Maiden-Mother's prayer
Beseeches at Thy throne of grace
Mercy before the Father's face.

Be near us, Angel from the skies,
Whose name God's healing signifies;
All ills of flesh take thou away,
Bring health to souls from truth that stray.

Ye ninefold ranks of angel-choirs
Whose order for our help conspires,
All past and present ills dispel,
From future danger guard us well.

Drive far away in shamed disgrace
From Christian lands the faithless race:
That so the rule one Shepherd hold
Over one flock, one single fold.

To God the Father praise be done,
Who hath redeemed us through His Son;
Anoints us by the Holy Ghost,
And guards us by the Angel-host. Amen.

PRAYER OF THE CHURCH IN HONOR OF ST. RAPHAEL ARCHANGEL

Vouchsafe, O Lord God, to send unto our assistance Saint Raphael the Archangel: and may he, who, we believe, evermore standeth before the throne of Thy Majesty, offer unto Thee our humble petitions to be blessed by Thee. Through Christ our Lord. Amen. (Roman Missal) An indulgence of three years. A plenary indulgence under the usual conditions, when this prayer has been said every day for one month. (Preces et Pia Opera," 414.)

NOVENA IN HONOR OF ST. RAPHAEL

V.   O God, come to my assistance.

R.   O Lord, make haste to help me.

Glory be to the Father, etc.

(The Versicle and Response are to be repeated every day.) Then continue:

O Christ, Splendor of the Father, Life and Strength of the heart, in the presence of the Angels we celebrate Thee by our prayers and hymns, uniting our voices with their melodious concerts. We praise with reverence all the celestial Princes, but especially the Archangel St. Raphael and faithful Companion by whose power the devil was enchained.

O Christ, King full of goodness, by this guardian remove far from us all the wickedness of the enemy; purify our hearts and our bodies, and by Thy sole clemency, introduce us into Paradise. In harmonious concerts let us give thanks to the Father, glory to Jesus Christ and to the Comforter, God three in One, living before all ages. Amen.

Hail Mary, etc., St. Raphael, pray for us.

The following Versicle and prayer are added on the **ninth day:**

V.   Pray for us, St. Raphael.

R.   That we may be made worthy of the promises of Christ.

Let us pray: O God, who to Tobias, Thy servant, when on his journey, didst give blessed Raphael the Archangel, for companion; grant that we who are also Thy servants, may likewise be safeguarded by his watchfulness, and be made strong by his help. May he who we faithfully believe ever to stand before Thy Majesty, offer up our prayers to be blessed by Thee. Through Jesus Christ, Our Lord. Amen.

PRAYER TO ST. RAPHAEL

O glorious Archangel, St. Raphael, great Prince of the heavenly court, illustrious for thy gifts of wisdom and grace, guide of those who journey by land or sea, consoler of the afflicted, and refuge of sinners: I beg thee to assist me in all my needs and in all the suffering of this life, as once thou didst help the young Tobias on his travels. And because thou art the 'Medicine of God," I humbly pray thee to heal the many infirmities of my soul, and the ills which afflict my body, if it be for my greater good. I especially ask of thee an angelic purity, which may fit me to be the temple of the Holy Spirit. Amen.

LITANY OF ST. RAPHAEL

(for private use)

Lord have mercy on us,
Christ have mercy on us,
Lord have mercy on us,
Christ hear us,
Christ graciously hear us,
God the Father of Heaven, have mercy on us,
God the Son, Redeemer of the world, have mercy on us,
God the Holy Ghost, have mercy on us,
Holy Trinity, One God, have mercy on us,

Holy Mary, Queen of Angels, *
Saint Raphael,
St. Raphael, filled with the mercy of God,
St. Raphael, perfect adorer of the Divine Word,
St. Raphael, terror of demons,
St. Raphael, exterminator of vices,
St. Raphael, health of the sick,
St. Raphael, our refuge in all our trials,
St. Raphael, guide of travellers,
St. Raphael, consoler of prisoners,
St. Raphael, joy of the sorrowful,
St. Raphael, filled with zeal for the salvation of souls,
St. Raphael, whose name means: Medicine of God,
St. Raphael, lover of chastity,
St. Raphael, scourge of demons,
St. Raphael, in pest, famine and war,
St. Raphael, Angel of peace and prosperity,
St. Raphael, endowed with the grace of healing,

Pray for Us

St. Raphael, sure guide in the paths of virtue and sanctification,
St. Raphael, help of all those who implore your assistance,
St. Raphael, who wert the guide and consolation of Tobias on
his journey.
St. Raphael, whom the Scriptures thus praise:—
"Raphael, the holy Angel of the Lord was sent to cure,"
St. Raphael, our advocate,

Pray for Us

Lamb of God who takest away the sins of the world, spare us,
O Lord.
Lamb of God who takest away the sins of the world, graciously
hear us, O Lord.
Lamb of God who takest away the sins of the world, have mercy
on us.
Christ hear us,
Christ graciously hear us.

V.	Pray for us, St. Raphael, to the Lord our God.
R.	That we may be made worthy of the promises of Christ.

Let us pray: Lord Jesus Christ, at the prayer of the Archangel
St. Raphael, grant us the grace to avoid all sin and to persevere in
every good work, until we reach our heavenly country, Thou who
livest and reignest world without end. Amen.

PRAYER TO ST. RAPHAEL

O God who in Thy ineffable goodness hast rendered blessed
Raphael the conductor of thy faithful in their journeys, we humbly
implore Thee that we may be conducted by him in the way of salvation, and experience his help in the maladies of our souls. Through
Jesus Christ, Our Lord. Amen.

PRAYERS TO ST. RAPHAEL THE ARCHANGEL FOR EMIGRANTS

I.	Saint Raphael the Archangel, thou wast a faithful com-
panion to the young man, Tobias, on his long journey from Syria
to Media, rescuing him from many dangers and, in particular, from
the danger of death in the river Tigris; we beseech thee with all our
hearts to be a safeguard and an Angel of consolation to our dear
ones on the long journey which they must undertake in order to
remove to foreign lands; do thou keep them far from all dangers
of body and soul, and grant that they may come in safety to the
haven of their desire.

Glory be to the Father, etc.

II. Saint Raphael the Archangel, arriving in Media thou didst bestow upon the young man, Tobias, extraordinary favors, going thyself to the city of Rages to receive the money from Gabelus, and causing him to find a worthy spouse in Sara, when she was delivered from the slavery of the demon, and enriching him with the goods of fortune; look, we humbly beseech thee, upon our dear ones who find themselves in foreign lands; do thou in like manner extend unto them thy heavenly protection, prospering their labors to the benefit of our beloved families and saving them from the many snares which will be laid for their souls, so that they may be enabled to preserve the precious gift of faith and to conform their lives to its teaching.

Glory be to the Father, etc.

III. Saint Raphael the Archangel, who faithful to thy mission didst bring back safe and sound to Syria, the young man, Tobias, enriching his house with blessings and graces, and even restoring the gift of sight to his blind father; ah, fulfill thy task in behalf of our dear emigrants. Bring them back in thine own good time, safe and sound, to our dear families, and grant that their return may be a source of consolation, prosperity and every choice blessing; and we, too, like the family of Tobias, will thank thee for all thy tender care and will unite ourselves to thee in praising, blessing and thanking the Giver of every good and perfect gift. Amen.

Glory be to the Father, etc.

V. Pray for us, Saint Raphael the Archangel,
R. That we may be made worthy of the promises of Christ.

Let us pray: O God, who didst give Thy blessed Archangel Raphael unto Thy servant Tobias to be his fellow-traveler; grant unto us, Thy servants, that the same may ever keep us and shield us, help us and defend us. Through Christ our Lord. Amen.
(Indulgence of 300 days once a day. 'Preces et Pia Opera," 619.)

PRAYERS TO ST. RAPHAEL AND THE HOLY ANGELS FOR TRAVELERS

May the Almighty and merciful Lord direct us on our journey; may He make it prosper, and maintain us in peace.

May the Archangel Raphael accompany us along the way, and may we return to our homes in peace, joy and health.

Lord, have mercy on us! Jesus Christ have mercy on us! Lord, have mercy on us!

PRAYER: O God, who didst cause the children of Israel to traverse the Red Sea dryshod; Thou who didst point out by a star to the Magi the road that led them to Thee; grant us, we beseech Thee, a prosperous journey and propitious weather; so that, under the guidance of Thy holy angels, we may safely reach that journey's end, and later the haven of eternal salvation.

Hear, O Lord, the prayers of Thy servants. Bless their journeying. Thou who art everywhere present, shower everywhere upon them the effects of Thy mercy; so that, insured by Thy protection against all dangers, they may return to offer Thee their thanksgiving. Through Jesus Christ, Our Lord. Amen.

ANOTHER PRAYER FOR TRAVELERS

O Almighty and merciful. God, who hast commissioned Thy angels to guide and protect us, command them to be our assiduous companions from our setting out until our return; to clothe us with their invisible protection; to keep from us all danger of collision, of fire, of explosion, of fall and bruises, and finally, having preserved us from all evil, and especially from sin, to guide us to our heavenly home. Through Jesus Christ, our Lord. Amen.

BEFORE STARTING ON A JOURNEY

My holy Angel Guardian, ask the Lord to bless the journey which I undertake, that it may profit the health of my soul and body; that I may reach its end, and that, returning safe and sound, I may find my family in good health. Do thou guard, guide and preserve us. Amen.

PRAYER TO ST. RAPHAEL, ANGEL OF HAPPY MEETINGS

O Raphael, lead us towards those we are waiting for, those who are waiting for us! Raphael, Angel of Happy Meetings, lead us by the hand towards those we are looking for! May all our movements, all their movements, be guided by your Light and transfigured by your Joy.

Angel Guide of Tobias, lay the request we now address to you at the feet of Him on whose unveiled Face you are privileged to gaze. Lonely and tired, crushed by the separations and sorrows of earth, we feel the need of calling to you and of pleading for the protection of your wings, so that we may not be as strangers in the Province of Joy, all ignorant of the concerns of our country.

Remember the weak, you who are strong—you whose home lies beyond the region of thunder, in a land that is always peaceful, always serene, and bright with the respendent glory of God. Amen.

MASS FOR THE FEAST OF THE HOLY GUARDIAN ANGELS

INTROIT. Ps. cii. 20. Bless the Lord all ye His angels: you that are mighty in strength, and execute His word, hearkening to the voice of all His orders. Ps. Bless the Lord, O my soul, and let all that is within me praise His holy name. Glory be to the Father, etc.

COLLECT. O God, who in Thine ineffable providence, hast sent Thy holy angels to watch over us: grant, we humbly pray, that we may always be defended by their protection and may rejoice in their fellowship for evermore. Through our Lord.

EPISTLE. Exod. xxiii. 20-23. Lesson from the Book of Exodus. Thus saith the Lord God: behold, I will send My angel, who shall go before thee, and keep thee in thy journey, and bring thee unto the place that I have prepared. Take notice of him, and hear his voice, and do not think him one to be contemned, for he will not forgive when thou hast sinned, and My Name is in him. But if thou wilt hear his voice, and do all that I speak, I will be an enemy to thy enemies, and will afflict them that afflict thee, and My Angel shall go before thee.

GRADUAL. Ps. xc. God hath given His angels charge over thee, to keep thee in all thy ways. In their hands they shall bear thee up, lest at any time thou dash thy foot against a stone. Alleluia, alleluia. Ps. cii. Bless the Lord, all ye His hosts: you ministers of His that do His will. Alleluia.

GOSPEL. Matt. xviii. At that time: The disciples came to Jesus saying, "Who then is the greatest in the kingdom of heaven?" And Jesus called a little child to Him, set it in the midst of them, and said: "Amen I say to you, unless you be converted and become as little children, you will not enter into the kingdom of heaven Whoever, therefore, humbles himself as this little child, he is the greatest in the kingdom of heaven; and whoever receives one such little child for My sake receives Me. But whoever causes one of these little ones who believe in Me to sin, it were better for him to have a great millstone hung around his neck, and to be drowned in the depths of the sea. Woe to the world because of scandals! For it must needs be that scandals come; but woe to that man by whom scandal does come! And if thy hand or thy foot is an occasion of sin to thee, cut it off and cast it from thee! It is better for thee to enter life maimed or lame, than having two feet, to be cast into everlasting fire. And if thy eye is an occasion of sin to thee, pluck it out and cast it from thee! It is better for thee to enter into life with one eye, than having two eyes, to be cast into the hell of fire. See that you do not despise one of these little ones; for I tell you, their Angels in heaven always behold the Face of My Father in heaven."

OFFERTORY. Ps. cii.   Bless the Lord, all ye His Angels; you ministers of His that execute His work, hearkening to the voice of His orders.

SECRET.   Receive, O Lord, the gifts which we bring Thee in honor of Thy holy Angels; and grant, in Thy mercy, that by their unceasing watchfulness we may be delivered from present dangers and may attain unto everlasting life. Through our Lord, etc.

COMMUNION. Dan. iii.   All ye Angels of the Lord, bless the Lord: sing a hymn and exalt Him above all forever.

POSTCOMMUNION.   We have received, O Lord, Thy Divine mysteries, rejoicing in the festival of Thy holy Angels; by their protection, we beseech Thee, may we ever be delivered from the wiles of our enemies and guarded against all harm. Through Our Lord, etc.

HYMNS FROM THE OFFICE OF THE HOLY GUARDIAN ANGELS

Praise we those ministers celestial
Whom the dread Father chose,
To be the guardians of our nature frail
Against our scheming foes.

For since that from his glory in the skies
The apostate angel fell,
Burning with envy, evermore he tries
To drown our souls in hell.

Then, hither, watchful Spirit, bend thy wing,
Our country's guardian blest!
Avert her threatening ills, expel each thing
That hindereth her rest.

Praise to the glorious Trinity, whose strength
This mighty fabric sways,
Whose glory spreads beyond the utmost length
Of everlasting days. Amen.

Ruler of the dread immense!
Maker of this mighty frame!
Whose eternal providence
Guides it, as from thee it came.

Low before Thy throne we bend;
Hear our supplicating cries;
And Thy light celestial send
With the freshly dawning skies.

King of kings, and Lord most high!
This of Thy dear love we pray:
May Thy Guardian Angel nigh,
Keep us from all sin this day.

May he crush the deadly wiles
Of the envious serpent's art,
Ever spreading cunning toils
Round about the thoughtless heart.

May he scatter ruthless war
Ere to this our land it comes;
Plague and famine drive away,
Fix securely peace at home.

Father, Son, and Holy Ghost,
One eternal Trinity!
Guard by Thy Angelic host
Us who put our trust in Thee. Amen.

PRAYER TO ALL THE GUARDIAN ANGELS

O pure and happy spirits whom the Almighty selected to become the Angels and Guardians of men! I most humbly kneel before you, to thank you for the charity and zeal with which you execute this commission. Alas! how many pass a long life without ever thanking that invisible friend to whom they owe a thousand times its preservation!

O charitable Guardians of those souls for whom Christ died! Flaming Spirits, who cannot avoid loving those whom Jesus eternally loved, permit me to address you on behalf of all those committed to your care, and to implore for them all in general a grateful sense of your many favors, and also the grace to profit by your charitable assistance.

O Angels of those happy infants, who as yet "are without spot before God," I earnestly conjure you to preserve their innocence.

O Angels of youth, conduct them, exposed to so many dangers, safely to the bosom of God, as Tobias was conducted back to his father.

O Angels of those who employ themselves in the instruction of youth, animate them with your zeal and love, teach them to emulate your purity and incessant view of God, that they may worthily and successfully co-operate with the invisible Guardians of their young charges.

O Angels of the clergy "who have the eternal Gospel to preach to all nations" present their words, their actions and their intentions to God, and purify them in that fire of love which consumes you.

O Angels of the missionaries who have left their native land and all who were dear to them in order to preach the Gospel in foreign fields, protect them from the dangers which threaten them, especially from contact with ferocious animals and poisonous snakes; console them in their hours of depression and solitude and lead them to those souls who are in danger of dying without baptism.

O Angels of infidels and pagans whom the true faith has never enlightened, intercede for them that they may at least open their hearts to the rays of grace, respond to the message delivered by God's missioners, and acknowledge and adore the one true God.

O Angels of all who travel by air, land or water, be their guides and companions, protect them from all dangers of collision, of fire and explosion, and lead them safely to their destination.

O Guardian Angels of sinners, charitable guides of those unhappy mortals whose perseverance in sin would embitter even your unutterable joys, were you not established in the peace of God, oh, join me, I ardently beseech you, in imploring their conversion.

And you, O Guardian Angels of the sick, I entreat you especially to help, console and implore the spirit of joy for all those who are deprived of health, which is among God's most precious gifts to man. Intercede for them that they may not succumb to despondency or lose by impatience the merits they can gain in carrying with resignation and joy the cross which Jesus Christ has laid upon them as a special token of His love.

O Angels of those who at this moment struggle in the agonies of death, strengthen, encourage and defend them against the attacks of the infernal enemy.

O faithful Guides, holy Spirits, Adorers of the Divinity! Guardian Angels of all creatures! Protect us all, teach us to love, to pray, to combat on earth, so that one day we may reach heaven and there be happy for all eternity! Amen.

NOVENA TO THE HOLY ANGELS

O all ye holy Angels, who contemplate unceasingly the uncreated beauty of the Divinity, in company with our ever glorious Queen, we present and offer to you this novena not only as a means of obtaining favors (here specify your request), but also as a reparation for our past ingratitude, and that of all men. Deign to accept it, O amiable Spirits, in union with the love and devotion of such saints as were especially devout to you, and obtain for us the grace to spend this life fervently that it may be the commencement of that blessed life which we hope to live forever with you in haven.

O God, who with wonderful order hast regulated the functions of angels and men, grant that those who always assist before Thy throne in heaven may defend our lives here on earth, through Jesus Christ, Thy Son, our Lord, who liveth and reigneth with Thee, in the unity of the Holy Ghost, one God, world without end. Amen.

LITANY OF THE HOLY ANGEL GUARDIAN

(for private use)

Lord, have mercy on us.
Christ, have mercy on us.
Lord, have mercy on us.
Christ, hear us.
Christ, graciously hear us.
God the Father of heaven, have mercy on us.
God the Holy Ghost, have mercy on us.
Holy Trinity, one God, have mercy on us.

Holy Mary, Queen of Angels,
Holy Angel, my guardian,
Holy Angel, my prince,
Holy Angel, my monitor,
Holy Angel, my counselor,
Holy Angel, my defender,
Holy Angel, my steward,
Holy Angel, my friend,
Holy Angel, my negotiator,
Holy Angel, my intercessor,
Holy Angel, my patron,
Holy Angel, my director,
Holy Angel, my ruler,
Holy Angel, my protector,
Holy Angel, my comforter,
Holy Angel, my brother,
Holy Angel, my teacher,
Holy Angel, my shepherd,
Holy Angel, my witness,
Holy Angel, my helper,
Holy Angel, my watcher,
Holy Angel, my conductor,
Holy Angel, my preserver,
Holy Angel, my instructor,
Holy Angel, my enlightener,

Pray for Us

Lamb of God who takest away the sins of the world, Spare us, O Lord.

Lamb of God who takest away the sins of the world, Graciously hear us, O Lord,

Lamb of God who takest away the sins of the world, Have mercy on us.

Christ, hear us.
Christ, graciously hear us.

Lord, have mercy on us.

V. Pray for us, O holy Angel Guardian,
R. That we may be made worthy of the promises of Christ.

Let us pray: Almighty, everlasting God, who in the counsel of Thy ineffable goodness hast appointed to all the faithful, from their mother's womb, a special Angel Guardian of their body and soul; grant that I may so love and honor him whom Thou has so mercifully given me, that, protected by the bounty of Thy grace and by his assistance, I may merit to behold, with him and all the Angelic hosts, the glory of Thy countenance in the heavenly kingdom. Who livest and reignest, world without end. Amen.

MEMORARE TO OUR ANGEL GUARDIAN

Remember O holy Angel, that Jesus, the eternal Truth, assures us you "rejoice more at the conversion of one sinner than at the perseverance of many just." Encouraged thereby, I, the last of creatures, humbly entreat you to receive me as your child, and make me unto you a cause of true joy. Do not, O blessed Spirit, reject my petition, but graciously hear and grant it. Amen.

PRAYER TO THE GUARDIAN ANGEL

O Angel! who by God's goodness has charge over me, who assists me in my necessities, who consoles me in my troubles, who obtains for me continually new favors, I thank you most sincerely. Gentle Guardian, continue your charitable care; defend me against my enemies, put away from me all occasions of sin, make me obedient to your inspirations and faithful to follow them, especially in my present difficulty (here mention your request). In the presence of Jesus Christ and the whole court of Heaven, I choose you for my protector, my defender, my guide and my advocate. I beg you to govern my whole life: my memory, understanding, will, inclinations, and desires. O Holy Angel, I love you, and wish to love you always. A thousand times I bless the Lord for the heavenly gifts with which He has adorned you, for the graces with which He has sanctified you, and for the glory with which He has crowned you. Guard and guide me now and at the hour of my death. Never leave me unprotected until you have brought me safe to Heaven. Amen.

ASPIRATION

O my dear Angel Guardian, preserve me from the misfortune of offending God.

A PRAYER TO THE GUARDIAN ANGEL

O Angel of God, my blessed protector, to whose care I have been committed by my Creator from the moment of my birth, unite with me in thanking the Almighty for having given me a friend, an instructor, an advocate, and a guardian in thee. Accept, O most charitable guide, my fervent thanksgiving for all thou hast done for me; particularly for the charity with which thou didst undertake to accompany me through life; for the joy with which thou wert filled when I was purified in the waters of Baptism; and for thy anxious solicitude in watching over the treasure of my innocence. Thou knowest the numberless graces and favors which my Creator has bestowed on me through thee, and the many dangers, both spiritual and temporal from which thou hast preserved me. Thou knowest how often thou didst deplore my sins, animate me to repentance, and intercede with God for my pardon. Ah! why have I so little merited a continuance of thy zealous efforts for my salvation? Why have I so often stained my soul by sin, and thereby rendered myself unworthy of the presence and protection of an angel, of so pure a spirit as thou art, who never sinned? But as my ingratitude and thoughtlessness have not lessened thy charitable interest for my salvation, so neither shall they diminish my confidence in thy goodness, nor prevent me from abandoning myself to thy care, since God Himself has entrusted thee with the charge of my soul. Penetrated with sorrow for the little progress I have made in virtue, though blessed with such a Master, and sincerely determined to correspond in future with thy exertions for my salvation, I most earnestly entreat thee, O protecting spirit, to continue thy zealous efforts for my eternal interest; to fortify my weakness, to shield me from innumerable dangers of the world and to obtain by thy powerful prayers that my life may rather be shortened, than that I should live to commit a mortal sin. Remember, O most happy spirit, that it was one act of profound humility, and one transport of ardent love for thy Creator, that caused God to establish thee forever in glory; obtain that those virtues may be implanted in my soul, and that I may seriously endeavor to acquire docility, obedience, gentleness and purity of heart. Conduct me safely through this world of sin and misery; watch over me at the awful hour of my death; perform for my soul the last charitable office of thy mission, by strengthening, encouraging, and supporting me in the agonies of dissolution, and then, as the angel Raphael conducted Tobias safely to his father, do thou, my good angel and blessed guide, return with me to Him who sent thee, that we may mutually bless Him, and publish His wonderful works for a happy eternity. Amen.

TO OUR GUARDIAN ANGEL

By Saint Gertrude

O most holy Angel of God, appointed by Him to be my guardian, I give thee thanks for all the benefits which thou hast ever bestowed on me in body and in soul. I praise and glorify thee that thou didst condescend to assist me with such patient fidelity, and to defend me against all the assaults of my enemies. Blessed be the hour in which thou wast assigned me for my guardian, my defender, and my patron. In acknowledgment and return of all thy loving ministries to me from my youth up, I offer thee the infinitely precious and noble Heart of Jesus, and firmly purpose to obey thee henceforward, and most faithfully to serve my God. Amen.

RECOMMENDATION TO ONE'S GUARDIAN ANGEL FOR A HAPPY HOUR OF DEATH

By Saint Charles Borromeo

My good Angel: I know not when or how I shall die. It is possible I may be carried off sunddenly, and that before my last sigh I may be deprived of all intelligence. Yet how many things I would wish to say to God on the threshold of eternity. In the full freedom of my will today, I come to charge you to speak for me at that fearful moment. You will say to Him, then, O my good Angel:

That I wish to die in the Roman Catholic Apostolic Church in which all the saints since Jesus Christ have died, and out of which there is no salvation.

That I ask the grace of sharing in the infinite merits of my Redeemer and that I desire to die in pressing to my lips the cross that was bathed in His Blood!

That I detest my sins because they displease Him, and that I pardon through love of Him all my enemies as I wish myself to be pardoned.

That I die willingly because He orders it and that I throw myself with confidence into His adorable Heart awaiting all His Mercy.

That in my inexpressible desire to go to Heaven I am disposed to suffer everything it may please His sovereign Justice to inflict on me.

That I love Him before all things, above all things and for His own sake; that I wish and hope to love Him with the Elect, His Angels and the Blessed Mother during all Eternity.

Do not refuse, O my Angel, to be my interpreter with God, and to protest to Him that these are my sentiments and my will. Amen.

PRAYER TO OUR LADY, QUEEN OF ANGELS

A Bernardine Sister was shown in spirit the vast desolation caused by the devil throughout the world, and at the same time she heard the Blessed Virgin telling her that it was true, hell had been let loose upon earth; and that the time had come to pray to her as Queen of the Angels and to ask of her the assistance of the heavenly legions to fight against these deadly foes of God and of men.

"But my good Mother," she replied, "you who are so kind, could you not send them without our asking?" "No," Our Lady answered, 'because prayer is one of the conditions required by God Himself for obtaining favors." Then the Blessed Virgin communicated the following prayer, bidding the Sister to have it printed and distributed:

AUGUST QUEEN OF HEAVEN! Sovereign Mistress of the angels! Thou who from the beginning hast received from God the power and mission to crush the head of Satan, we humbly beseech thee to send thy holy Legions, that, under thy command and by thy power, they may pursue the evil spirits, encounter them on every side, resist their bold attacks and drive them hence into the abyss of eternal woe. Amen.

BIBLIOGRAPHY

All About the Angels, Father Paul O'Sullivan
Butler's Lives of the Saints
Catechism of the Council of Trent
Catechism of Perseverance
Devotion to the Nine Choirs of Angels, Abbe Boudon
'Neath St. Michael's Shield, Benedictine Sisters, Clyde
Our Heavenly Companions, Benedictine Sisters, Clyde
The Precious Blood, Father Faber
The Spirit World About Us, Father Husslein, S.J.
Verses, Cardinal Newman
Why Is Thy Apparel Red, Father Walz, C.PP.S.

THE JUDGMENT

If you have enjoyed this book, consider making your next selection from among the following . . .

Prices subject to change.

Prices subject to change.

Prices subject to change.

At your Bookdealer or direct from the Publisher.
Toll-Free 1-800-437-5876   **Fax 815-226-7770**

Prices subject to change.

NOTES

NOTES

NOTES

NOTES

NOTES